FIGHTING CLOWNS of HOLLYWOOD

With Laffs by **THE FIRESIGN THEATRE**

A Memoir by
DAVID OSSMAN

© 2018 by David Ossman

Laffs © 1979, 1980, 1981, 2017
by Phil Austin, Peter Bergman, David Ossman, Phil Proctor
The Firesign Theatre

Editing & Archival research by TFT's Archivist, Taylor Jessen.

Costume photographs by Jerry De Wilde (1979) and Barrie M. Schwortz (1980)

Fighting Clowns scratchboards and FT's 1980 logo by Bruce Litz

Nick Danger Third Eye logo by William Stout

Nick Danger Ripoffs from Google

A tip of the Firesign Fedora to my Editor, Ben Ohmart!
And one to Valerie Thompson, designer of all our books!

ALL RIGHTS RESERVED.

No part of this book may be reproduced in any form or by any means, electronic, mechanical, digital, photocopying, or recording, except for in the inclusion of a review, without permission in writing from the publisher.

Published in the USA by:
BearManor Media
P.O. Box 71426
Albany, Georgia 31708
www.BearManorMedia.com

Printed in the United States of America.

ISBN: 978-1-62933-298-7 (alk. paper)

CONTENTS

MORE THAN FOREWORD . . . 1

WHAT WERE WE FIGHTING ABOUT? . . . 5

CHAPTER 1: NICK DANGER RETURNS . . . 7

CHAPTER 2: THE OWL & OCTOPUS SHOW . . . 27

CHAPTER 3: BEN BLAND'S ALL-DAY MATINEE . . . 49

CHAPTER 4: THE HISTORY OF THE ART OF RADIO . . . 65

CHAPTER 5: FROM BRECHT, VIA WILLIE THE SHAKE,
TO JOEY'S HOUSE WE GO . . . 81

CHAPTER 6: MANY MEANWHILES . . . 135

CHAPTER 7: THE ODYSSEY . . . 197

CHAPTER 8: A NEW AMERICAN PAGEANT . . . 213

CHAPTER 9: SAUCER! . . . 229

CHAPTER 10: THE HORRIBLE TOUR . . . 235

CHAPTER 11: THE PINK HOTEL . . . 245

CHAPTER 12: WASHIINGTON, D.C. . . . 263

AFTERWORD . . . 267

MORE THAN FOREWORD

If there were justice and sanity in the world, The Firesign Theatre would today be as goddy as Monty Python. Quentin Jerome Tarantino would be ripping these guys a new career by having Ossman and Proctor playing guards in an overlong and wordy scene in his latest space epic. Nick Danger would still be alive. And radio (and comedy albums) would be the new TV which everyone would ignore in front of their scrolling pocket computers.

Because these guys Rock.

AND Roll.

And I can't say enough about their contribution to comedy. They've been around 50 years and around the block and yet, listening to their albums — group and solo stuff both — they are as dated and timeless and hilarious as a Goon Show.

In fact, I got to be a laconic FT fan from the opposite end. After I found Monty Python on MTV, which led me to *The Goon Show*, which led me to sketch comedy, I found their superb *Shoes for Industry!* compilation CD set at Tower Records in the early 1990s. I was heavily into The Jerky Boys then, and still ignored all the *many* stand-up comedy albums out there, because I'm into dialogue, man. I love to write it (for Fred Frees, etc.) and I *love* to listen to it. When I was a kid of 11, I found Jack Benny and Fibber McGee and Molly LONG, *long* after any kid of 11 should have liked anything that wasn't visual, and The Firesign Theatre opened up a whole new kind of audio comedy right there for me. It was like watching *Airplane!* in your head. It was something so funny, there's no way you can laugh at everything the first time, because there's just too much of it. You *have* to watch *Airplane!* 20 more times. You *have* to listen to FT 22 more times if you want to get All the juices down your bib. There's such a pace and layerness to their comedy that even a Ted Ray or Robin Williams is going to do a double take and have to rewind.

David's book here pays a great tribune to that brilliance by doing the thing that's most important for this homage: loading it down with at-the-moment journal entries, and scripts. Especially the stuff you've never heard before. And some of this was cut? I can't believe it. It's better than the average *Simpsons* episode. And I never watch *The Simpsons*.

David and I both share a love of Spike Milligan and absurdism and illiterature that has perhaps gone out of fashion in today's Will Ferrell world. That's why it's all the more important that a book like this exists, straight from the lion's mouth, and I'm honored as hell to be a part of it.

I still don't understand why the remaining two FT members aren't under million dollar contracts to the most expensive comedy shows being made today. Here's hoping this book will change all that. Justice, sirs.

"Surely you don't doubt my obvious insincerity?" — Bloodnok

BEN OHMART
SEPTEMBER 2017

THE FIGHTING CLOWNS OF HOLLYWOOD
AUSTIN, OSSMAN, BERGMAN, PROCTOR

WHAT WERE WE FIGHTING ABOUT?

By the end of the Nixon-saturated Kissenrockafordafeller decade, with The Eighties looming, gasoline available only on alternate days of the week, inside pages of newspapers reporting the various threats of polar-icecap-melting, acid rain, carbon dioxide, electronic smog, aerosol sprays and, yes, even the eventual collapse of the universe itself, The Firesign Theatre once again became a theatre and raised the curtain on the sorry state of the United States.

In January 1979 when we began our work together, the CIA's pseudo-Shah of Iran (a LIFE Magazine kinda guy) fled to Panama, the absolutist Ayatolla Khomeini took over and by April ancient Persia had become an Islamic Republic. Worse, by year's end, fifty Americans were being held hostage in Teheran and "American patience was wearing thin."

Worse and worse in the meantime — in July, Saddam Shame took over in Iraq. Need I say more? Foreshadowing? Yes! The Sandinistas grabbed Nicaragua the same month and shortly inspired the Iran-Contra spectacular. (The good news was, the Sony Walkman took power at about the same time, freeing your music and our laffs from the hi-fi.)

In December the Soviet "Union" (Remember them? They hated each other!) invaded Afghanistan and President Jimmy Carter, the "killer rabbit"-haunted, Gospel-totin' Georgia peanut farmer, signed on to secretly aid those noble and trusty Afghan opium farmers in their centuries-old battle against everybody else.

In view of the threat of Apocalypse Pretty Soon, The Firesign Theatre took as its slogan for 1979 "The idea is to make people laff." OK, let's get it on . . .

CHAPTER 1
NICK DANGER RETURNS

January 1979. It was all about Nick Danger, our decade-old 1940s radio detective character, at that moment in The Firesign Theatre's suddenly re-booted creative life. "*Producers are talking about Clouzot-type series, pos w/C Chase as the star,*" I wrote in my January journal notebook ("college ruled," with Farrah's right nipple on prominent display on the cover).

Nick, an almost-afterthought that helped make The Firesign Theatre's second LP a success, spoofed the radio stereotype of the hard-boiled detective and the medium itself, spinning off laffs that shortly entered the language of burgeoning young boomers. ("What's all this brouhaha?" was my contribution.) Nick seemed pretty easy to understand, compared with the Joycean layers of the record's other side, "How Can You Be In Two Places At Once, When You're Not Anywhere At All?"

The Firesign's LA beginnings, late 60s-early 70s, when three of us lived in historic Mixville, North of the Other End of Sunset, on the fringes of Downtown, did our thing at Columbia Records on Sunset, KPFK on Cahuenga and The Ash Grove down on Melrose, had run its course after five intense years. Though we would always remain brothers of a sort, it seemed then like it might help to get some distance on the collaboration. Especially since the collaboration had been split by the absence of Proctor & Bergman, suddenly off on their own in 1972.

I moved with my wife Tinika to orchidaceous Santa Barbara, ninety miles up the Coast from the my partners — the three loveable Hollywood Clowns — in what was still a beach town in 1971, with a stop-light on the freeway. By 1979 I'd been commuting from home to Los Angeles for Firesign and other professional business on and off for eight years.

(Our last LA apartment was on a hill overlooking Echo Park and the encroaching metroplex with its rising skyscrapers, LAPD 'copter searchlights and deadly smog. The KDAY radio towers just behind us leveled so much "effective radiated power" into the place that the kitchen stove literally vibrated with Top 40 hits. Our landlord was "Jaws" himself, Richard Kiel, only scary if you encountered him unexpectedly.)

In January 1979 I was in the midst of teaching my first Radio Drama class to students at UCSB and readying a performance of the 1950 Hollywood noir movie "Sunset Boulevard" in a live radio version. I was applying for my first NEA grant — like Santa Barbara, a far cry from Hollywood.

When the call came in early January with a possible radio syndication deal, I made the drive South into LA. Firesign wrote at night, at Peter's temporary house, a Benedict Canyon bungalow with a lot of decorative painting and woodwork on the façade, making it over into a pseudo Swiss chalet with piles of dead leaves on the miniature just-off-the-road frontage. It was wintery. Bergman announced, "It was so cold I froze my jalapenos!"

We quickly delivered the first five episodes of a new 3-minute "drop-in" Nick Danger radio series — a "pilot," of course — and recorded all ten pages on the night of January 15th. It was now raining heavily in L.A. Which seemed appropriate for Nick, or for any other hard-working LA dick.

It had been ten years since we were in CBS studio B, recording the original "Nick Danger" for our second Columbia LP. And here we were again, in the Future, in Hollywood and in the studio with a silly script (originally titled "The Adventure of the Maltese Shoe") and our great new organist, Richard Parker, replacing the late and much missed David Grimm, who had brought musical life to the original.

Pleasant circumstances (I wrote in my journal, here in italics) — *3 mikes in a smallish room, but that presented no problems. Scripts ready and looked good — 2 hour runthru*

Peter Bergman, Phil Proctor, Phil Austin at Peter's, Jan. 1979

rehearsal & then about 3 hours of recording. All went smoothly at every stage of the session — PP excellent w/SFX, PA a controlled ND, w/good character, PB being echoic & full of bits of future business — seemed typical as I remember to have him projecting as much as being here-and-now.

Remember, we hadn't worked in the studio together for three or four years and the above is an on-the-spot assessment of where our careers might be as Firesign, in the Future. Peter, of course, being there in the Future already, as much as on-the-job, as it were.

All acting went well & no arguments — an observer remarked that he'd never seen anything like it — hadn't heard a 'no' all night. Engineers also put us in a class by ourselves — & I felt we belonged there. Rich Parker quiet and terrific as usual, w/great timing.

So it was done — a real anniversary event — & it made me feel good.

NICK DANGER & THE ADVENTURE OF THE MISSING SHOE

EPISODE ONE

MUSIC: NICK DANGER THEME

ANNOUNCER: And now — The Future Adventures of Nick Danger, America's ONLY detective. Brought to you by your local Chevrolet bottler. This week, Nick walks into — "The Adventure of the Missing Shoe."

MUSIC: ORGAN STING

NICK: I was sitting in my dingy office/apartment, waiting for my heart to start beating. And the two eggs I had boiling on my hotplate stared at me like . . . two eggs. I knew how they felt. Hard boiled. I poured myself an eye-opener — a shot of Old Crow in an eye-cup.

SFX: POURING

NICK: And tossed it back. (GULP) Ow! My eye! I leaned back in my swivel chair and propped my dogs on my empty desk.

SFX: PHONE RINGS

NICK: (TO HIMSELF) Just a second!

SFX: RING

NICK: Where is my left shoe!!

SFX: RING — PICKUP PHONE

ROCKY: (ON PHONE FILTER) So you've noticed!

NICK: Who — is this?

ROCKY: (ON FILTER) Who's THIS?

NICK: They call me — Danger.

ROCKY: (FILTERED) Oh. Sorry, wrong number.

SFX: PHONE DISCONNECT

MUSIC: ORGAN STING!

ANNOUNCER: We'll be right back to Nick Danger, after this.

ANNOUNCER 2: Brought to you by Poon's Farm Sausage — cut from real Belgian waffle-fed Poon's Farm Porkers. It's a bland continental blend of old spiced meat and today's shredded newspapers. From Pork to Nuts, it's got to be — Poon's Farm!

ANN: And now, back to "The Future Adventures of Nick Danger."

MUSIC: ORGAN THEME UP

NICK: I traced the call. The wire led from my phone through the office wall to a pole, placed suspiciously close to my window — and from there to another . . . and another . . . and another . . . and another . . . then — right through the wall of the phone company.

SFX: CRASH

NANCY: Hello, sir. Can I help you? I'm your service representative, Nancy.

NICK: (INTERIOR VOICE) What a tomato!

NANCY: What?

NICK: Perhaps you can tell me where this phone cord leads to?

NANCY:	Which one?
NICK:	T̲h̲i̲s̲ — one! (GRUNTS)
SFX:	DISTANT PHONE FALLS TO FLOOR
ACME:	(MUFFLED, FROM BEHIND DOOR) Who pulled the phone off my desk?
NANCY:	It's a wildman with one shoe, Mr. Acme!
SFX:	DOOR OPENS
ACME:	Come in, Mr. Danger. I've been waiting for you...
MUSIC:	ORGAN STING
ANNOUNCER:	The Firesign Theatre's Nick Danger will be back tomorrow, when the script says... "FOOTSTEPS...DOOR OPENS...TWO SHOTS!!"
SFX:	FOOTSTEPS...DOOR OPENS...ONLY ONE SHOT...
MUSIC:	ORGAN STING AND OUT

EPISODE TWO

MUSIC: NICK DANGER THEME

ANN: And now, the Future Adventures of Nick Danger — America's only detective. This week, Nick stumbles along through "The Adventure of the Missing . . .

SFX: RUSTLING PAPER

ANN: . . . "Page!" . . . I mean "Shoe!"

MUSIC: ORGAN STING

NICK: (INTERIOR VOICE) Yesterday, I lost my shoe. And now I find myself in the office of Alexander Graham Acme, the inventor of the phone company.

ACME: Pull up a Chair Phone, Danger, and put your foot where your mouth is.

NICK: (INTERIOR VOICE) This heel had no soul. He got a kick out of booting people around. (ALOUD) OK, Acme, I'll play your game, but — what's in it for me?

ACME: More money than you've ever seen in your life!

NICK: That can't be much.

SFX: INTERCOM BUZZER

NANCY: (ON FILTER) Emergency call for you, Mr. Acme.

SFX: PHONE CONNECT

ROCKY: (ON PHONE FILTER) Boss! Boss! I did like you told me. I called that dumb dick, Danger from the shoe-store and . . .

ACME: Ah — I think you've got the wrong number, Rococo.

NICK: (INTERIOR VOICE) Rococo — that sleazy weasel! Where had I heard that voice before?

ROCKY:	(ON FILTER) Yesterday, Danger!
NICK:	What?
MUSIC:	ORGAN STING
ANN:	We'll be right back to Nick Danger, after this!
ANNOUNCER 2:	Brought to you today by "Ma Rainey's Wholesome Moleskin Cookies."
VOICE:	I've heard of 'em.
ANN 2:	Yes, the whole moleskin cookie in the oilskin bag. Each cookie is a whole mole — won't melt in your hand, or in your mouth — they go right through ya! Not messy! That's "Ma Rainey's Whole Moleskin Cookies." Eat 'em, wipe 'em off, eat 'em again — your first bag will be your last! "Ma Rainey's" for a rainy day!
MUSIC:	DANGER THEME
ANN:	And now back to the Future Adventures of Nick Danger.
NICK:	Hold it, Acme! There's something fishy here!
ACME:	You're right. (SNIFFS) It's your sock, fishfoot!
NICK:	You're gross, Acme.
ACME:	My gross?
SFX:	PAPER RUSTLE
ACME:	Last year — twenty billion dollars before taxes! And I never pay taxes! I'm the wealthiest man in the city — and I have to walk around like this!
SFX:	FOOTSTEPS (THUMP — PAUSE — THUMP, ETC.)
NICK:	(INTERIOR VOICE) Either Acme was only wearing one shoe or there was something seriously wrong

	with our sound effects man! This caper's gonna take more than two episodes to solve!
MUSIC:	ORGAN UP
ANN:	The Firesign Theatre's Nick Danger will be back tomorrow, when we hear Nick say . . .
NICK:	Where are those writers?
MUSIC:	ORGAN UP AND OUT

EPISODE THREE

MUSIC: NICK DANGER THEME

ANNOUNCER: And now, the Future Adventures of Nick Danger — America's ONLY detective. Today, Nick trips over a clue to "The Adventure of the Missing Shoe."

MUSIC: ORGAN STING

NICK: All right, fellas, what've you written for me today?

WRITER: You see, Monday you were missing a shoe.

NICK: Great, good.

WRITER: Yesterday, Acme was missing a shoe.

NICK: Tough. So what?

WRITER: Well, you see, today, you and Acme . . .

NICK: Nah. I don't like it! The girl! What happened to the girl?

WRITER: The girl? OK, great! That's great! OK, Nick, how's about this . . .

SFX: TYPEWRITER

WRITER: "Nick limped back to the office, only to find the girl waiting for the flatfoot (FADING) breastlessly . . .

NANCY: Hello, Nick.

NICK: Something told me you'd be here.

NANCY: Betcha it was two bald writers with glasses.

NICK: Ha ha ha. Speaking of glasses, baby — there's a pair in my drawers. Let's get down to business.

NANCY: Oh, Nick!

MUSIC:	ORGAN UP — AND OUT (!)
ANN:	(WHO HAS BEEN PLAYING NANCY, STILL IN FALSETTO) We'll be back to Nick Danger (REGAINS HIS REGISTER) after this . . .
ANN 2:	Today, Nick Danger is brought to you by this question:
VOICE:	"It drives people mad, but it makes quieter engines."
ANN 2:	That isn't a question.
VOICE:	Well, that's not an answer!
ANN 2:	There is no answer! And here in the many arms of Octoglomorate "We ask the questions that can't be answered — today."
VOICE:	(SLIDING FROM HIGH TO LOW REGISTER) From changing voices . . .
ANN 2:	To stre-e-e-tching hearts!
MUSIC:	ORGAN UNDER
ANN 2:	Count on Octoglomorate!
ALL:	1 — 2 — 3 — 4 — 5 — 6 — 7 — 8! Octoglomorate!
ANN:	And now, back to the Future Adventures of Nick Danger.
MUSIC:	ORGAN STING
NANCY:	I'm scared, Nick.
NICK:	Don't worry, I've had this operation . . .
NANCY:	What?
NICK:	Never mind . . .
NANCY:	But I do mind, Nick! Like a puppy! I'll do anything you say . . .

NICK:	Sure. Sit. Roll over and fetch my shoe!
NANCY:	(BARKS) Oh! Oh! Oh! I can't find your shoe, Nick, but I do have this "darned sock!!"
SFX:	SOCK!
NICK:	Ooooooh!
SFX:	BODY FALL
MUSIC:	DANGER THEME UP
ANN:	Tune in again tomorrow to The Firesign Theatre's Nick Danger, when the script says:
NICK:	Oh, my head! Wait'll I get my hands on those writers!

MUSIC UP AND OUT

EPISODE FOUR

MUSIC: NICK DANGER THEME

ANN: And now — The Future Adventures of Nick Danger, America's ONLY detective. This week, Nick shuffles endlessly on through "The Adventure of the Missing Shoe!"

MUSIC: MYSTERIOSO UNDER

NICK: (INNER VOICE) When I finally returned to what I laughingly call "consciousness," I was staring at the back of my eyes. My ears were working, but I couldn't believe what I was hearing.

COP 1: More shoes in the closet, sir.

COP 2: (OFF) There's some in the drawers, too.

COP 1: Looks like there's more than an ounce of shoes here for sure, Lt. Bradshaw.

COP 2: He even tried to floor some Flusheims down the toilet!

COP 1: And look at this sir, in the lining of his coat!

COP 2: Ugh! Baby shoes!

BRADSHAW: Baby shoes?! That does it! I'll kill 'im! Wake him up!

MUSIC: ORGAN CLIMAX AND OUT

SFX: SLAPPING AND GROANING

NICK: Hey, cut it out! Save the rough stuff for your girl-friends, ya lugs.

BRAD: We got you this time, Danger. You really stepped into it, flatfoot!

NICK: I'm not a flatfoot, Bradshaw, I'm a gumshoe — you're a flatfoot!

BRAD:	I'll kill 'im! I'll kill 'im!
SFX:	BRIEF STUGGLE
COP 1:	Take it easy, Lieutenant!
NICK:	Look, I can explain everything. See, I had this girl . . .
BRAD:	Congratulations. Sorry I haven't got a cigar.
NICK:	A girl who socked me with a shoe! This is a frame.
BRAD:	And it's not a pretty picture, Danger! We're takin' you downtown.
NICK:	On what charge?
BRAD:	"Grand Theft Left Shoe." Let's go.
MUSIC:	ORGAN UP
ANN:	We'll be back to Nick Danger in a minute.
ANN 2:	Brought to you today by the United States Post Office Cheese Club of Skink, Wisconsin. Once a year, the People of Skink are milked by the Government, the milk put into parcels, and mailed to you. And by the time it reaches YOU — its cheese!
ANN:	This month's President Ford Commemorative Cheese Flag — Honduras! Don't miss it! Sign up today at the Food Stamp line at your neighborhood post office!
ANN 2:	And now, back to "The Future Adventures of Nick Danger."
MUSIC:	UP AND UNDER
SFX:	FOOTSTEPS ON STAIRS
NICK:	(INNER VOICE) Bradshaw and his boys were draggin' me down to the Bureau of Missing Shoes. I had to clear myself, but time was running out — and so was

	I! (ALOUD) Say, Bradshaw, I just noticed — your one loafer's untied.
BRAD:	My loafer? Oh, yeah, thanks.
SFX:	FIGHT AND GROANS, FOOTSTEPS RUNNING, VOICES FADE OFF IN BG
NICK:	(INNER VOICE) I hotfooted it down the street and hopped into a handy cab! (ALOUD) If ya gotta shoe on, step on it, cabby!
ROCKY:	Sure. Sit back and relax, Mr. Danger.
NICK:	Oh, no! Rococo!
SFX:	CAR PULLS AWAY
ROCKY:	LAUGHS!
ANN:	Be sure to listen again tomorrow, when we hear Danger say . . .
MUSIC:	DRAMATIC UNDER
SFX:	CAR UNDER
NICK:	Where are you taking me, waffle-eyes?
ROCKY:	Tune in tomorrow, Danger, and you'll find out! Hehehehehehe!
MUSIC:	STING AND OUT

EPISODE FIVE

MUSIC:	NICK DANGER THEME
ANN:	And now, The Future Adventures of Nick Danger — America's only detective. Today, Nick laces up "The Adventure of the Missing Shoe."
MUSIC:	DRAMATIC UNDER
SFX:	CAR UNDER, THEN THE HISS OF GAS
NICK:	(INNER VOICE) Acme's grubby gunsel Rococo had me bagged in the back of a cab filled with...laughing gas. Ha, ha, ha! It was a cheap way for the writer's to grab a gag, but this wasn't funny! (LAUGHS UNCONTROLLABLY) There was $6.50 on the gas meter of the cab as we pulled into an abandoned Phone Company warehouse... (GASPING) So that's the plot! Fresh air... (RECOVERS) Unregistered aliens turning left shoes into phones. Now for our gag!
MUSIC:	UP AND OUT
ACME:	Take the gag out of his mouth, Rococo.
ROCKY:	Right, Boss.
NICK:	Thanks. Now I can stop thinking!
NANCY:	Want me to hose him again, Mr. Acme?
ACME:	Certainly not, Nancy, my dear. Today, he's our special guest.
NICK:	I just left a grilling — what's this? A roast? What's at stake here?
ROCKY:	You'll loin soon enough.
NICK:	Stop it! You're making me hungry!!
MUSIC:	ORGAN STING

ANN:	We'll be back to The Future Adventures of Nick Danger . . .
MUSIC:	PATRIOTIC UNDER
ANN 2:	But first, here's a special message from the inventor of the phone company, Alexander Graham Acme . . .
ACME:	Hel-lo, Americans. Call me "Joe." Here's some good news. The Phone Company is sending every one of you a big brown bag of hot food! Why? Because we took your shoes away without telling you. Why not? We knew you'd ask. And that's why we didn't tell you. And now, they're coming back — with bells on 'em!
SFX:	RING RING
ANN:	That's right. The Phone Company has turned your left shoe into a phone. Yes, it looks like a phone, but it's as durable and reliable as your old shoe. It IS your old shoe! Walk on it — talk on it. (PHONE RINGS) For you, from The Phone Company!
MUSIC:	STING AND OUT
ACME:	Get it now, Danger? Every time you take a walk, you make a call.
NICK:	Which means you make a penny out of every loafer in town!
ACME:	Right. They foot the bill and Crime Marches On!
ROCKY:	Shall I give it to him now, Boss?
ACME:	Sure, Rocky.
ROCKY:	OK, Danger. Ugh! Here's your bag of hot food.
NANCY:	And here's your shoe, Nick.
SFX:	PHONE RING

ACME:	If the shoe fits — answer it.
NANCY:	I'll get it for you, Nick.
SFX:	DANGER FALLS DOWN
NICK:	Take it off my foot first, Nancy. Here.
NANCY:	Hello? Yes — I'll tell him. Nick?
NICK:	Yes — Nancy . . . ?
NANCY:	It was the writers. They . . .
NICK:	What?
NANCY:	They want me to hit you again.
MUSIC:	STING AND UNDER
NICK:	(INNER VOICE) It was all over. There was nothing left for me to do but limp back to my office in my two-tone touch-tones.
SFX:	TOUCH-TONES UNDER
NICK:	It took hours! Every seven steps, you make a call. And then, once in a while, you get one.
SFX:	PHONE RINGS
NICK:	I got it!
SFX:	NICK FALLS
NICK:	Gotta remember to take the shoe off . . . Hello?
VOICE:	(PHONE FILTER) Hello? I wanta order a anchovy to go, and hold the pizza.
NICK:	Hold the pizza? Sorry, buddy. You've got the wrong number. I spell my name DANGER!
MUSIC:	NICK DANGER THEME IN AND UNDER

ANN:	Tune in again next week for The Firesign Theatre's "Future Adventures of Nick Danger," created by Philip Austin, Peter Bergman, David Ossman and Philip Proctor. Until next week this is your announcer, Fraud Thursby, saying — goodbye?
MUSIC:	UP AND OUT

THE NICK DANGER CAST

ROCKY   BRADSHAW   NICK   THE ANNOUNCER

This little script and the sweet studio performances re-acquainted us and made us laugh together, always sez the Reader's Digest, "the best medicine." It would have been fun to do a season's worth of new episodes, each enriching the Nick Danger legend, but that never happened. Like so many Hollywood deals (Chevy Chase as Nick Danger?) it didn't so much as fall through as vaporize.

The next job came a couple of weeks later. No "deal," baby, this was the real rock 'n' roll scene!

CHAPTER 2
THE OWL & OCTOPUS SHOW

The owl and the octopus went to see
In the pussycat's pea green boat
They took their Sony and plenty of money
Wrapped up in a frog-skin coat

On the first of February 1979 I got a call from Phil Austin to say we had been invited to play The Roxy — a busy rock club on the Sunset Strip — a two-day gig in a month to six week's time. *So things are heating up.* On the 10th of February, a Saturday, Bertolt Brecht's birthday (also Jimmy Durante's and William Blake's) I was up and into LA at 9 am, up a very narrow branch of Benedict Canyon to Peter's place — he wasn't home, and I waited on the Chalet porch. The mood was Raymond Chandler. I was reading "Farewell, My Lovely" for the umpteenth time.

P[roctor] & B[ergman] were full of promises & maybes — lots of action — very dazzling & really overwhelming. Phil had the drop on 'em tho, by handing out $675 checks for the Roxy show at the beginning. I believe they might have almost turned it down, were it not for the check & the attendant "deals." These involve ABC (a P&B pilot 'featuring TFT'), Lorimar — a movie they thought of called, god forbid, 'Spaced Out' starring us — we're not only America's only comedy group, but also have the lock on how to make teeners laugh. All this thanks to P&B's "Americathon."

"Americathon" was based on a sketch, "Gothamathon," by Proctor & Bergman — one of several extended pieces they had performed on the road. It was a good idea — a telethon to raise funds for a broke USA — but P&B never got to write the screenplay and worse, they weren't even in the movie. It opened in August to a hearty thumbs down from Roger Ebert. It did not lead to Firesign's much-anticipated film career.

We finally got down to the Roxy & P[hil] A[ustin] was loaded for bear — he'd recorded AM TV & had the tape & what HE wanted to do was to start in the morning ("A Day In The Life") & go on etc. Well, I argued Betamax & got put off. We agreed on most things tho, w/PB getting less involved as the aft drifted away from his business & got down to the real work. I chimed in some of my "old material," got good laughs & felt OK — I have my notes too, & next time I'll come down with the tape.

Phil's "A Day on TV" notion was a classic Firesign organizing idea — the TV day would begin with a generic "Morning Show." I really wasn't much interested in satirizing those AM people again and besides, in arguing for the Betamax I was trying to keep up with technology (ha! ha!) and time-delay watching (oh, well). Here's what I really thought — and feared:

Entering the H'wood World — in a way — that image of me as Joe Gillis — here it comes — now if only I don't end up in the pool.

I threw the I Ching about the forthcoming Roxy Show on Thursday, February 15. "Biting Through — energetic overcoming of obstacle to union." The changing line was 9 in the 4th place, "Bites on dried gristly meat. Receives yellow arrows." Looked like trouble was on the way. "It is necessary to be as hard as metal and as straight as an arrow to surmount the difficulties." Well, I'd do my best.

On Friday I drove down to L.A. for a day-long writing session — *we worked hard & did abt 6 pp of material — all early AM TV — had a good time together.* We put in another full day on Saturday — *talked a lot at the beginning this time — & more theory & opinion came out — in pleasant ways.*

1979 was the year of the family sit-com, with "Three's Company" and "The Jeffersons" in the Top-10 and "Happy Days" close behind. "The Love Boat" was big and the Bubba Set had "Dallas" and "Dukes of Hazard." We could do that. It also brought TV by satellite — USA, ESPN, TMC — and HBO, in its infancy, broadcasting nine hours a day. We'd have good old, slightly boozy Ben Bland (me) to host our all-the-time-everywhere movie channel and maybe we'd find a dummy or blow-up "person" to extend the cast.

We came up with a *FLASHY OPENING:*
4 of us in night clothes wake and all go to & turn on 4 different TV sets — all in

unison — go back to sit in chairs & each be the first thing we see — 4 different channels, then we all get up and dial/tune into one and speak at the same time.

Right! Everybody's watching TV. What happens, we asked, when anybody and everybody is THE ACTUAL CAST on their televisions? We live in that future now, Dear Friends — the World of the Screen, where we're lonely digits on the Isle of Selfie. Reality, media's 21st Century drug, has brought us to a terrifying Future.

When I think this is the 1st all new piece of FT writing since E[verything] Y[ou] K[now] nearly 5 years ago — well! We stopped late in the day — I think everyone was surprised at how long we kept at it — did a few more pages.

At first we'd agreed on a new version of "Exorcism In Your Daily Life," a sort of educational-film-sit-com combine and a new Nick Danger "movie." Those embedded in a day of television programming. Perhaps we could have a *Live news report from a place with no light.*

Our Hell Probe news story was inspired by a spate of planetary exploration events beginning with two probes fired into Venus in December 1978. On March 5, 1979, Voyager 1 arrived at Jupiter and sent back incredible photos. It flew on to arrive at Saturn on July 9th. Pioneer 11 finally got to Saturn at the end of August. Saturn pretty much looked like Hell from this angle. (Typical of us to flip Heaven — Space — and Hell — down there.) Skylab, now a happy orbiter, was first announced from the cover of TIME in mid-June. Space wuz da place.

In 1979, Viet Nam was embroiled in a little war with China. The triumphant new Communist government ordered all ethnic Chinese out, which led to an exodus by boat. The first "boat people" were being admitted to the U.S. as we were writing. Eventually over 800,000 Southeast Asians were transplanted here. (There were Cuban and Haitian "boat people" too — how could a sit-com be far behind?)

A week later, February 23rd, I returned to L.A. where writing on the Roxy script continued. I spent a lot of time with Peter after the writing session and *we stayed up late on coffee & black label discussing Nick Danger.* It was always wise to have an idea to kick off the writing and we needed one now.

At sometime or another Austin and I had cobbled up a story about Nick Danger going off to the Army in 1940 and returning to find out that he, Nick, was being played by another actor (not that Nick was an actor, of course) in a successful movie series. Nick returns from the War to find his identity stolen. Interesting premise?

I brought the subject up at the Sat am mtg & PB proceeded to outline the story (PA's and mine) — PA was amazed! PP bought the whole thing & only pulled one little temper thing in the disc[ussion]. Felt broken thru, & spent the aft on writing a ND movie section for the TV piece — now tent. titled A Season In Hellivision.

It was another week before I returned to L.A., arriving in town on a Summery Monday. We re-wrote, going over the script that I'd typed, did another four pages on Tuesday, continued on Wednesday and Thursday before I returned to Santa Barbara and its small-town social whirl. When I got back to the City the next Wednesday I spent a *full day working on costumes & getting all the parts finally sorted out — went smoothly. Ready to rehearse tomorrow.*

A lot of show-biz talk was going on — the undermutter accompanying plans for the Roxy appearance. Unfortunately, it tended to pull the group apart instead of knitting us more firmly together. The Proctor & Bergman duo had created Austin and Ossman (and we'd done a couple of touring stage shows together three or four years before) but gnawed away at the roots of the basic Firesign collaboration. I wrote about my partners in my journal:

PA is fixing his sights on the ND movie as the next project. He is also strong behind the ND radio synd (only PB expresses nervousness abt "the time to do it.") but that seems now to be as remote as the late Summer for a Fall start. Otherwise PA in his confidential exchanges w/me is optimistic & full of good words — the old combination of suspicion & superiority is a natural under-current but no longer the outward manifestation of Phil's thoughts and actions.

P&B are into negotiating the deal, but I have my doubts (along w/PA) that it's actually going to happen — it and all the other P&B projects are either commercial "comedy writing" jobs or "1-page ideas" for comedy TV. Nothing is currently happening in the real world, but there is a lot of blue-sky.

Our group appearance in this new piece may have great influence on all their connections — if we are as effective as in the past, it ought to create a demand — or else scare everybody away.

Peter himself sits on the edge — between P&B and TFT, between businessman & intellectual, avant-gardist & social progressive. He is enthusiastic about Carter these days — unhumorously. He toasted "our eternal friendship" & I'm sure he meant it. He is sane and responsible, but always at the edge of one sort of excess or another.

PP remains bull-headed & undiplomatic in that Leo manner, but he's less egocentric in many ways.

The checks and balances of the writing sessions have been very reminiscent of the pre-'72 days, but only of the smoothest ones. Form seems more readily sensed by the group & no one has as many "moral" holdouts as they used. There is only a bit of extraneous chit-chat & it's usually not just a delaying exercise.

It remains to be seen what The Owl & Octopus Show really is — it's just a script & some funny costumes now. A piece abt TV? Abt the Am. Family in the '80s? Where does it come in our work? (FT II as PB calls us — this is that group's 1st work.)

The great horned owl is the mascot of this chalet. Outside — in Terra Linda — the streets are full of octopuses.

About those squids and octopi — the Southern California coast had just been "invaded" by tons of Humboldt squid. The Pacific was full of them and the beaches well and truly slimed with the creatures, which can get up to twenty pounds. Not a unique occurrence, the squid have invaded again and again, most recently in January 2013. When it happens, local news has endless on-the-spot coverage.

It was mid-March now and still rainy, with a brush of snow on the mountains beyond the Hollywood Hills. We took our scripts and costumes to The Roxy and spent a long day on rough-blocking the 1st half of O&O Show. PP got so "angry & frustrated" at one point he had to leave to calm down. And w/the rest of us so obviously laying back & being cooperative — yet firm. Poor Phil — donno what it is in his makeup that gets him so anxiety-ridden when working w/TFT.

Fri a much easier day — began w/an interview w/a guy from [U]SC, then we much more easily staged the 2nd half of the piece & wrapped up about 4 — ready to start a week of rehearsals.

The piece got better as we worked on it in the rehearsal — tying things up here & there & bringing in the "family" theme together at the end.

We had a party at the Austin's on Friday night: *It was a remarkable occasion — the first reunion of the Old FT. I think we were all much amazed at both the durability of the association, but at the new piece — written for stage and TV — a total departure in past approach. No old material. A play abt The Family.*

There was only time for a quick trip home to Santa Barbara — home of the ur-reality show, "An American Family," filmed there in 1971 and scandalously aired everywhere in 1973 — before plunging back into the Hollywood scene. This time I chose not to stay at Peter's Swiss Chalet, but signed in at the Tropicana on Santa Monica Boulevard. It isn't there anymore, but it was for twenty years home to rockers, wanna-bes, and scene-makers. The Police were there when I arrived — the band, not the cops — and a great breakfast was served family-style at Duke's, a coffee shop below the rooms. *Kinda spare — nothing on the walls, but*

quiet and close to everything. We rehearsed four days at the Groundlings stage, finally getting a run-through on Friday. It was exhausting. After another day's work we headed for The Roxy itself and a Noon call. Very exciting.

The Roxy had once been a Sunset Strip strip club called the Largo. It reopened for rock in 1973. (Lou Adler, Grammy-winning record producer, was one of the new owners and brought the Rocky Horror Show from London to the Roxy stage that year.) By 1979 the venue was infamous, but sported lots of lights and good sound.

We were billed as "The Entire Firesign Theatre" and appeared in between gigs by Firefall and Dire Straits.

Sunday — a long day beginning at noon at the Roxy — setup, lights, costumes etc — we got our walk-thru very late — just set the lights — no run-thru — we did have a line run-thru in the afternoon & all seemed ok.

The 1st Sunday show ran over 2 hours and we quickly cut back between shows. The 2nd show didn't go up until after midnight & it was 3 am by the time we got out. The shows were ok — essentially dress rehearsals — but the reaction was good from the opening night crowd.

Unbelievably, the Owl & Octopus Show opened with 44 distinct pieces in 64 pages and I personally played 22 different characters, all with their own costumes, eyeglasses and props. It was an explosion of ideas going in too many directions. We cut more and more.

The Monday night show was very much better — sharper. We continued cutting and trimming on both shows — still running 2 hrs & out very late. Once again the aud was very good — sell-out shows — & they stayed w/us. The content of the show began to come very clear — owls, octopuses & all.

Tuesday night I was very tired & my voice was going. In spite of more cutting the show still ran 1:50. 1st show sold out or nearly & even the very late 2nd show had a large audience. Exhausted, we left for home as soon as we could — 3 am — drove thru an incredible rain in the Valley, stopped at T. Naylor's in 1000 Oaks for coffee & food to go & finally got home at 5 am.

Pennsylvania atomic plant out this week — in the news tonight. Israel/Egypt Peace signed last weekend. Five Mile Island! Wait a minute! Didn't we just see "China Syndrome?" Things looked bad again.

From the original scripts of the O&O Show, I've reconstructed some of the segments that were dropped from the much-tightened "Joey's House," which would play the Roxy in July. It did start with a dang Morning Show . . .

"THIS MORNING NOW"

OLD LADY ENTERS, BOTTLE IN HAND. SHE TURNS ON THE TV AND WATCHES "THIS MORNING NOW."

OLD MAN IS DISCOVERED ON STAGE, IN A WHEELCHAIR. HE TURNS THE TV TO A RELIGIOUS PROGRAM.

SNIFFLES ENTERS AND TURNS THE TV TO "LUCY."

JOEY COMES IN AND SWITCHES THE TV FROM CHANNEL TO CHANNEL, FINALLY SETTLING ON "THIS MORNING NOW." THE OLD LADY IS THE VOICE OF THE NEWSPERSON, JANE.

JANE: . . . and it's Spring in California, even though it's still snowing here in New York — so these are the latest in Springtime California Fashions — they're pajamas! And they jog in them, they eat in them, they take meetings in them — they even sleep in them! There you have it, the latest crazy, lazy fad from kooky California. And it's six minutes before the hour, no matter where you are. And we'll be back, after this . .

BOB: Hi, I'm an actor, and when that camera gets close, close, close — it can break your teeth! (HE TAKES OUT HIS CHOPPERS) And that's what happened to me!

ANNOUNCER: That's right. Busy denture wearers like soap-opera stuntman Bob Dogge don't have time to clean their teeth each morning AND drink a whole, fulsome breakfast . . .

BOB: And that's why I and millions of my fans use FANG-TANG, the Instant Denture Breakfast.

ANNOUNCER: It's this easy — drop a tab on your teeth at bedtime . . .

BOB: FIZZ. YAWN.

MUSIC BRIDGE.

ANNOUNCER: Next morning, when you get up . . .

BOB: (YAWN) Drink it down. (HE DOES)

ANNOUNCER: Now! With special Sharpening Agents!

BOB: Look! My teeth are eating their way through the glass!!

ANNOUNCER: That's FANG-TANG, The Instant Denture Breakfast — from Octoglomerate.

JANE: We're back. It's four before the hour, and you know, it's often been said that it'll be a cold day in Hell before Gene sees something on his TV screen that he really likes. Well, we don't know exactly how cold — or hot — it's going to be in Hell today, but we do know that it's colder than hell outside our studio today, and I guess that means Gene has seen something he likes. So, here's Gene with the TV scene on your TV screen. Gene?

GENE: Thank you, Jane Plain. Well, at last, an intelligent docudrama in prime-time. It's called "Thank you Mr. President," and revolves around the character of Dominique Malfleur, a Haitian pastrycook and former White House slave, played by Suzanne Pleshette, who has learned to inhabit the body of Dwight David Eisenhower. Ike gets into trouble when his — or is it her? — special problem keeps her — or is it him? — from attending the National Kangaroo Trials across the street at Uncle Joe's. Vice President Nixon, played rather stiffly by the late Adolph Menjou, falls in love with Ike and his job, but Harry and Franklyn will have none of it, and arrange to send him — or is it her — or is it them? to Korea to end the war — or is it just a police action? It's a Hell of a show! A little over-written and a little over-lit, like all overly good television. I was glad that it was on and I was glad when it was over. I think you will be too. This is Gene on your TV screen with the TV Scene. It's four minutes before the hour, everywhere you see me. This is "This Morning Now."

TOM: In the next hour, Jane will let us in on a bold new product that will allow young people to stay even younger, forever. And I'll be talking to a Washington Economic Expert in a three-piece suit about things that we don't exactly know what to do about. Now, here's Dick with the Hell Watch Report.

DICK: Thanks, Tom. The Satan One Hell Probe, after its 666-day voyage, begins its descent today into "Hell" — or what scientists call "the lowest observable point in the Universe." Known traditionally as "an infernal abode of anguished souls in torment," Hell may turn out to be an important new source of molten mineral wealth. Satan One, we understand, is behaving as predicted by JPL Spokescreature Bob "Flash" Gordon. Temperatures down there are up to about 666 degrees — that's million — 666 million degrees and rising. And Tom, we'll keep a close watch on that story — they expect the first photometric data to come in around 4:35 this afternoon.

TOM: There will be some spectacular photos when the probe enters the atmosphere — if you can call that an atmosphere — before the equipment meltdown. It's two minutes before the hour. And we'll be back.

GOONS (SINGING) At gi-gi-gi-Gibberson's
The whole Shoot 'n' Scratch is yours!

GOBBER: Yes, it's Double-Dealing Deep Cut Dizzy Disco Daze at your convenient neighborhood Gibberson Disco Mart. Now, play the Hoot 'n' Scratch Game . . .

GOON: Who?

GIBBER: You! Scratch out the President's eyes and sniff your prize!

GOON: I won a whole half an octopus!

GIBBER:	Who?
GOON:	I did! At Gibberson's!
GOONS (SINGING):	Don't get mad! Don't get sad!
GIBBER:	Just look for the owl in a strait-jacket, spinning day and night over every store! You'll lose your grip on Reality at Gibberson's!
GOONS:	Where the whole shootin' scratch is yours!

"THE DEVIL'S PYRAMID"

BOB: All right!! That was absolutely terrific! What a great battle of the Super Monsters! And come on out Mrs. Presky, because — you're a winner!

MRS. PRESKY ENTERS

BOB: That's right, Mrs. Carolyn Presky, you bet on the right Monster and now let's see just what you've won — a 10,000-piece Digital Dinnerware set!! Your very own Light-Up Stucco Walls!! And half your weight in valuable Nuclear Wastes!! But it could all be taken away from you, Mrs. P — just like your house.

MRS P: I loved that house, Bob. My dog was in that house.

BOB: All right!! But now it's time to meet your Second Challenger on your way to the top of The Devil's Pyramid! He's come all the way from Bubba, Texas — let's give a big Devil's Pyramid welcome to — Harlan Plain!

HARLAN IS SPUN ON STAGE

BOB: How're ya doin', Harlan?

HARLAN: I'm OK.

BOB: Tell me — what do you do down there in Bubba?

HARLAN: Well, I enjoy lookin' carefully at pictures of nekkid women.

BOB: All right! Have you got any hobbies?

HARLAN: I enjoy dreamless sleep and, well, I'm a Reverse Baptist, so I like to watch TV.

BOB: All right! Are you ready to pick your categories as you try to lay the first golden cornerstone on your way to build the Devil's Pyramid? These are your choices — get ready, here they come! "Famous Dead Insects!"

HARLAN: There are no famous dead bugs . . .

BOB: Let's go to the next category then. Here we go — "Lost Negro Airmen!" How about that?

HARLAN: I thought there weren't any Negroes anymore . . .

BOB: All right!! Next — "Owls and Octopoids!" How about that?

HARLAN: That's meaningless! I know what I'll do. I'll take the wild card.

BOB: You mean you want to "draw," sucker?

HARLAN: I sure as hell do!

BOB: All right! (HE HANDS HARLAN A PISTOL) Here's your gun and here comes the Laser Kid!

A WESTERN-ATTIRED ROBOT SPINS ON

HARLAN: Wait a minute! I thought I was gonna play cards!

THE ROBOT SHOOTS AND WOUNDS HARLAN.

BOB: (LEADING AUDIENCE APPLAUSE) Well, you lost to the Laser Kid, Harlan. And that means the advantage goes to you, Mrs. Caroline Presky. You get to Pick Your Punch! Ready?

MRS P: You bet I am, Bob! I'm going to run this geek right down the royal ramp.

BOB: All right! What the Devil is it going to be?

MRS P: Drunk driving!

HARLAN: Oh, no!!!!!

BOB: All right! We'll bring on those fancy leather gloves and bonded bourbon right after this . . .

CLONE (WHISPERING): We're with Mrs. Peggy Koolzip in the Italian Dinner section of Super Karate Food Mart — the first 24-hour restaurant where YOU do the buying, but WE do the work! Tell me, Peggy, how do you like that Lasagna marinara?

PEGGY: Well, Mr. Clone, these Farina Shells were a real daytime buy at 69 cents — and your farm-fresh meat here couldn't be firmer or chewier at 2 dollars a pound off, with a pound of coupons. Even these little jars of oregano were under-valued at 19 a gram!

CLONE: That's a lot of enthusiasm, Peggy. Have you tried shopping elsewhere around town?

PEGGY: Oh, yes! But I always have to take the raw food home and cook it in hot water and fat for my late husband. And this is a lot better than sticky stamps and dirty dishes.

CLONE: What about regular family burger and chicken stops?

PEGGY: Well, I think there's so much more — waste — when you don't do your own shopping.

CLONE: Thanks, Peggy. How about it? Why don't you try us — now that just eating every day costs more than most of us can afford — KARATE FOOD MART — The Restaurant in a Super Market!

After the morning news and a channel-switch to a game show, starring one of our favorite characters, Mrs. Caroline Presky, it was time for the Soap, another favorite, "Lawyer's Hospital." This would have made a great continuing sketch for television if anyone in the business had been brave enough test it back then. Now it might make late-nite cable.

LAWYER'S HOSPITAL, EPISODE TWO

WITH MADGE AND MIDGE

MADGE: Midge, I give up! I can't get these stubborn chicken-oil stains out of Bob's underwear. And it's the only pair we've got!

MIDGE: Those chicken stains are alive, Madge. And to clean them, you've got to kill 'em — dead!

MADGE: What about my old detergent, Midge?

MIDGE: Feed it to your kid, Madge! Now there's new improved DIOXIDOL — with Secret "Agent Orange" — the Chemical Chicken Killer!

CUTS TO A NEW SCENE WITH "BOB" SERVING IN HIS UNDERWEAR

BOB: More chicken, ladies?

MIDGE: Madge, Bob's underwear smells wonderful!

MADGE: I "Owe it all to DIOXIDOL!"

COMMERCIAL MUSIC CROSSES TO SOAP OPERA ORGAN

BOB: (ON PHONE) Yes, yes. I understand, Dr. Dugong. Turk has regained feeling in his third leg. (TELLS MIDGE:) Turk has regained . . .

MIDGE: I heard.

BOB: Oh. What? Doreen tried to shut off her life support system? (TO MIDGE) Doreen tried to . . . oh, you heard. Did she succeed? (TO MIDGE) She didn't succeed!

MIDGE: That's terrible!

BOB: That's wonderful!

DON BAMBI: Oh, Midge! Come-a here for a secondo, would you, dearest? (SHE DOES) Midge, I'ma just receive thisa telegram, and she'sa say that Stu was apologize ina court yesterday for givin' Kay the mind-altering drugs! So, the only thing I cana do, isa pull off the hit-man and forgivea him for raping her.

MIDGE LOOKS CONFUSED

BOB: (STILL ON THE PHONE) Don Bambi? Don Bambi? Come here for a second, will you? (HE DOES) I'll tell him. Don Bambi, I've just been informed that Dr. Dugong has asked your little Nikki and big Nora to combine their child custody and cardiology projects. Aren't you proud of them?

DON BAMBI: I'ma only proud ofa one of them!

ELLIOT ENTERS AND LOOKS AT MIDGE

ELLIOT: Oh . . . Jumbo?

MIDGE: I'm . . . Midge.

ELLIOT: Good. You know, Jumbo, that Jerry goaded Seneca into hiring a mercenary in that palimony battle of the Dugong's over Mignon. You don't suppose that's why Margo told me that they'd substituted that dead rabbit for that poor little boy?

MIDGE: You mean, the little Gibberson boy I ran over this morning?

ELLIOT: Well, that would explain the skidmarks on his little tombstone.

BOB: Elliot! Elliot! Come up here for a minute, could you? (HE DOES) I've just been told by Dr. Dugong's lawyer that Midge's father told him that he told her that they'd been living in a flashback!

DON BAMBI: In my country, that woulda be a tragedy!

MIDGE: (EAVESDROPPING) I am? Am I? Oh, Midge, Midge, Midge! "Don't be sad, don't go mad! Don't go mad, don't be sad . . . " Don't lose your grip on reality!

	Find something familiar to relate to . . . Oh, my, Elliot! What a fabulous new lawn sprinkler! Where did you get it? At Fiogucci's?
ELLIOT:	I don't have a lawn, much less a lawn sprinkler.
BOB:	Hey! What are you two talking about? . . . Wait a minute! That's not a sprinkler! It's an octopus!

ORGAN STING AND MUSIC OUT

ITALIAN SINGER:	Ah! Ca — li — maaaaaa — ri! (ETC)
WINO:	Ever since I'ma was a liddle-a squid, I'ma wanna drinka the wine the color a the wine-dark sea! An' that's whya my mamma, she slip a fresha squid into the bottom ofa every bottle of — The Cabernet of Wino Calimari!
SINGER:	Ah! Ca-li-maaaaaaaa-ri!
WINO:	(DRINKS FROM THE BOTTLE) Good nose! Lottsa legs! And what a body! Don't be a sucker! Try it! The Cabernet of Dr. Calimari!
SINGER:	Ah! Calimarrrrrrrrr-iiiii!
WINO:	From Calimari Vinyards, Wino, California.
SINGER:	Ah! Ca-li—HIC!—maaaari!

This next show was always my favorite idea. Taking the "American Family" concept (I knew the "real" American Family, so-called) and turning it into a "news" program was so logical it took a new century to realize the potential and create the spectrum of intimate family realities that occupy the mouse holes of our multiple screens.

THE FAMILY HOUR NEWS

JACK: It's 6:30 and everybody's home. It's time for the Family Hour News, with TV's first family of newspersons — Harlan Plain, Sr., Cloaca Muffinose Plain, and Jack Plain, Jr. With Pearl Plain Charles and the twin Charles girls, Nicky and Nora. Now, here's my Dad . . .

HARLAN: Thanks, Jack, Jr. In the headlines tonight — Dad threatens to leave Mom after 35 years of married life. Octopuses clog sewers after heavy rains — Son estimates cleanup cost to his own Father at over one hundred dollars! And I find out some startling facts about Mom — at the Post Office! Mom . . .

CLOACA: Thank you, Dad. I'll have a special report on the family finances — what's left of them — plus the latest from Jack Jr.'s investigation of Dad's alleged infidelities. Dad will try and explain himself a bit later on, with a commentary on the day's events — "Only One Dad's Opinion." Midge?

MIDGE: You ought to leave him, Mom . . .

CLOACA: Oh, Midge!

MIDGE: I'll join the twins in a no-holds-barred discussion of their first overnight date, and then I'll have more on what it's like to be a newly divorced woman in the fast lane at the supermarket.

HARLAN: Thanks, Midge. Tonight's embarrassing stories coming up, but first let's talk about savings . . .

SFX: REVOLVER SPUN, TRIGGER CLICKS AGAIN TWICE

HARLAN: Ya know, the best half of life better be the last. This is Harlan Plain, Sr., and I'm talking to Austin "Pops" Feebler. Tell me, Pops, don't you think at your age it's a little bit dangerous to be playing Russian Roulette?

SFX:	SPIN, ANOTHER CLICK
POPS:	Heck, no, sonny! At this game I can be a winner 5 out of 6 times!
SFX:	SPIN, ANOTHER CLICK
HARLAN:	Yes, the Last Half has gotta be the best. So when your number comes up, make it an account number at the Valley of the Shadow Federal Savings.
POPS:	I'm still goin'! Wahoo!
SFX:	SPIN . . .

CHAPTER 3
BEN BLAND'S
ALL-DAY MATINEE

I loved playing Ben Bland. He was based on a real LA movie host, on films broken every couple of minutes for horrible commercials, on the ubiquity of old movies all-day-every-day on the local TV channels. Basically the same world that Ralph Spoilsport came from. Ben appeared first in a record album I was trying to save — "Just Folks" — which had been half built of old radio routines and needed some new, live material. Ben came along with a commercial about The 10 Danger Signals of Depression, which were, of course, the real thing. In the studio, recording Ben's continuity one night, Proctor arrived with a bottle of Mount Gay.

The two of us consumed most of the bottle as Ben rambled on for the record, getting drunker as the takes went on. Authenticity! I always gave Ben a coffee cup filled with a little something and a pile of confusing note cards. His show's producer — an off-stage voice, usually Peter — kept having to get Ben back on track, usually just by intoning "Ben!"

The "Men In Hats" script that follows is "Reel Two" of the convoluted story in which Nick has a serious case of Multiple Identity. But, turn up the volume! Here's Ben . . .

BEN: Hi, there! This is Ben Bland again on the old All-Day Matinee — back again for movie number two — a great second feature — a B-picture — now, you might wonder where that familiar expression came from — well, in the old days of pictures, right at the beginning of sound, the studios had these high-beam ceilings and the bees used to build . . .

VOICE OF BEN'S PRODUCER: Ben . . .

BEN: Right — but I'm glad you joined us for a fine old movie and a few hundred commercials. No? — well, I'm just kidding. We'll be eating a little something

	and drinking our cup of coffee with you while we watch one of Hollywood's award-winning finest — nominated for Best Hat Based On A Hat From Another Medium — it's called "Men In Hats" — a Nick Danger mystery thriller — I know you'll like that — and it stars Huston Bogus, Rex Spoffard and Betty Brent, and let's go to that right now ...
PRODUCER:	Ben!!
BEN:	The — uh — the Trivia Quiz today! Who was the real — now, I'm not talking about the original, not about the radio shows or movies or TV shows, but who was the REAL Nick Danger — the one they took it all from — that's a tough one. The phone numbers are on your screen. Enjoy them. Let's go on with the picture, please.

THE MOVIE ROLLS. IT APPEARS TO BE REEL 2.

BLOOTWURST:	(ENTERING) Chief! Chief!
BRADSHAW:	Don't over-do it, Blootwurst. I'm not the Chief yet. Just call me CAPTAIN Bradshaw.
BLOOT:	Yes, sir, Lieutenant. Sorry, I forgot.
BRAD:	What is it, Blootwurst?
BLOOT:	That's a good question, sir. My mother used to call it my "discovery stick."
BRAD:	Blootwurst!
BLOOT:	Yeah, she called it that, too. It does look like a little like a blootwurst.
BRAD:	Why don't you just go out and come in again?
BLOOT:	Oh, no-can-do, Chief. There's a guy outside who's trying to get in. He says his name is Nick Danger.
BRAD:	Nick Danger? The guy in the movies?

BLOOT:	He says he's a private dick.
BRAD:	Whaaaat?
NICK:	(INTERIOR MONOLOGUE) There was nothing I could do now. This was my last hope. I was nothing now, just another jerk with his hat in his hand and a story to tell the cops. So Bradshaw was a Captain — a big shot. I stared at the wall. The wall stared back. The clock ticked. Maybe I'd had too many blank stares today. Maybe I'd heard one too many pat answers. Maybe I didn't care anymore. Something inside me was trying to go to sleep. Something deep down didn't want to play the game Bradshaw's way. I didn't have a chance. I was beginning not to care about who the hell Nick Danger was.
GROGAN:	Whaddya say?
NICK:	Nothin' sweetheart, just thinking out loud.
GROGAN:	Well, ya better keep it down, citizen. Anything you think can be held against you.
NICK:	Anything you hold against me ain't worth thinking about.
GROGAN:	Sez you, mug!
BLOOT:	Chief is gonna see ya now, pal.
NICK:	Thanks for nothin', Blootwurst. Same lid, huh?
BLOOT:	Whaddayer talkin' about?
NICK:	The lid. The skimmer. Your hat, Blootwurst. Don't remember me, huh? You still skimmin' the till down at Maizies on Spring Street?
BLOOT:	Jesus! How did you know about that?
NICK:	C'mon, Blootwurst. You never change your M.O.

BLOOT: M.O.? I've never had M.O.! I use a good, clean, strong green soap — with the sharp, cutting smell of an Irishman in every bar.

NICK: Lissen, jerk! It's me — Danger! Back from the war!

BLOOT: I don't care if you're back from Hell! I never seen ya before in my life. Now, get in there and face the Chief!

BRADSHAW: What can I do for ya, soldier?

NICK: Don't call me "soldier" — the war's over, Al. It's me, Nick Danger.

BRAD: Yer not Nick Danger! I've seen the movie. What is this? Some kind of joke?

BLOOT: Ya want I should throw this joker out, Chief?

BRAD: Naw, I wanna grill this bird myself. Frisk him.

NICK: Gesundheidt.

BLOOT:	(PERFORMS AN INTIMATE SEARCH) He's clean, Chief. But I'm not. I've got to go take a shower. Where's my knife? (HE LEAVES)
NICK:	Look, Bradshaw . . .
BRAD:	Shaddup!
NICK:	It's me — Danger!
BRAD:	Shaddup!
NICK:	I got back from the Pacific a little late . . .
BRAD:	Shaddup!
NICK:	And everybody seems to have started the party without me . . .
BRAD:	Shaddup!
NICK:	I can't get a soul to recognize me . . .
BRAD:	Shaddup!
NICK:	Oh, they know Nick Danger alright . . .
BRAD:	Shaddup!
NICK:	Only I ain't him!
BRAD:	Shaddup!
NICK:	Seems they got some other guy in mind . . .

THERE'S A PAUSE, THEY LOOK AT EACH OTHER.

BRAD:	That's better. Have a drick, Nink.
NICK:	What?
BRAD:	Have a drimp, Lik. A dink, Rik. Shaddup! Everybody shaddup! I can handle this. Have a drink, Danger.

NICK: That's more like it, Al. I see you even remembered the brand.

BRAD: Sure, sucker. The A&P brand they burned on the bottom of my right heel. A&P — for Anselmo Pederasty.

NICK: Past history, Al. That case is just a warm memory now. Twelve bottles of the best. We drank 'em in Chinatown.

BRAD: You really screwed me on that caper, Danger. From behind my back.

NICK: Hey, water under the dam. Milk under the bridge. No use cryin' over spoiled metaphors.

BRAD: I ain't cryin', Danger — because I know you've got a problem. And you know I know you got a problem.

NICK: You mean about people pretending they don't know me?

BRAD: You know it. And now . . . I'm gonna screw you. Let's drink to the memory of Anlelmo Pederasty. Here's to ya, Noname!

HE THROWS HIS DRINK AT DANGER

NICK: Hey!

BRAD: Blootwurst! Get this crazy drunk outta here!

BLOOT: He smells like an Irish Bar. Come on, ya bum!

NICK: I'm Nick Danger! I'm . . .

NICK IS THROWN DOWN A FLIGHT OF STAIRS

BEN: Well, I didn't think I could — I didn't want to break into that scene — it's a good scene, and — as you know — it's from reel two. Well, I talked to my producer — and I'll tell ya what we're gonna do. We're just going to go on with the movie. And we'll show ya the first reel at the end — we think it's gonna make more sense to you that way, and — be a lot smoother.

And ya know — speaking of smooth — I'd like to talk to you about STUD SPRINGS — the men's-only Retirement RV Ranch. Men — are you aching to drag for giant catfish? Shoot golf or rats on a secret golf course the wives can't ever find? Dine on your own fresh meat killed on the highway and served flat at the Lodge? Dress how ya want, smoke pipes, even dance together in a nature-like wilderness of controlled boating adventures and hi-speed masculine fun. You've just got to find out more about it — it's all there, just waiting for you to make it possible.

Spend a long weekend searching for your vacation homesite and the many improvements — like: No house — nothing to clean! No roads — you won't need the car! No water — no pesky utility bills to pay — and no octopuses. Call — the numbers are still on your screen. No salesman will call if you call first. Or write for our 3-pound scenic brochure with our attractive models posed The Way You Like 'Em. Write STUD SPRINGS, in care of Wetpatch, Arizona 80666.

WE CUT AWAY TO A COMMERCIAL

KID: Mmmmmmm . . . ! Gee, Mom! These napkins taste just like your hamburgers used to!

CLOACA: My family trusts me — they'll eat anything I put on the table — including the napkins!

ANNOUNCER: Then we asked the former Cloaca Muffinose of Wetmop, Misconsin to tell us which they thought her husband would prefer — cardboard lunch plates with NAPKIN EXTENDER or a sizzling hot owl — fresh from the microwave.

CLOACA: Well, my husband is really into coke lately and he doesn't seem to have an appetite for anything.

ANN: That means more for you and the kids, Mom! So — having trouble making both ends meat? Just . . .

KID: Pile on the napkins!

ANN: NAPKIN EXTENDER! New from Octoglomerate.

WE CUT BACK TO THE STUDIO — BEN IS ON THE PHONE

BEN: . . . Orson Welles? On the radio? Yes, that's right — Orson did play him on the radio, but that's not the question we're asking today. I'll say this one more time, folks, what we want to know today is — who was the REAL Nick Danger? We'll try once more, later in the show. Now, this friendly word from the Handgun School of Truckstopping . . .

PRODUCER'S VOICE: No, Ben!

BEN: That's right — we want to remind you to tune in tonight at — what time is it? 8 o'clock tonight wherever

CHAPTER 3: BEN BLAND'S ALL-DAY MATINEE

	that might be in your time zone, for the Jerry Thomas-Danny Lewis Telethon for Musical Discophy . . . well, I guess we all gotta dance sometime . . .
PRODUCER:	Ben! Read it again!
BEN:	Right! That's Nuclear Disastrophy Disco telethon. Now, let's get back to our wonderful Nick Danger movie — "Men In Hats!"

WHEN WE REJOIN THE MOVIE, "NICK DANGER," PLAYED BY MOVIE STAR REX SPOFFARD, IS WATCHING HIS STUNT-DOUBLE UNDERGO A VIOLENT DEATH.

THE "STUNT DOUBLE" IS OUR OWN NICK DANGER.

REGGIE, THE DIRECTOR AND HIS ASSISTANT, ARCHIE, WATCH AS "DANGER" PANTOMIMES SNOOPING THEN IS SHOT SIX TIMES, STAGGERS AND FALLS.

ALL THIS ON A MOVIE STAGE AT PARANOID PICTURES. WE FOCUS ON THE DEAD BODY, THEN THE DIRECTOR CALLS:

REGGIE:	Cut! That was beautiful! Print it! Get up, you, get up! First team. Where's Rex? Rex, Rex, darling! We're ready for your scene . . .
ARCHIE:	First team! Mr. Spoffard — on stage!
NICK:	(INTERIOR MONOLOGUE) I knew I was in Hollywood now. These jokers were actually trying to make a movie out of our old friend, the Anselmo Pederasty case. And this skinny, limp-lipped English nancy was supposed to be me!
REGGIE:	Please, quiet, people! Now, Rex. In this scene . . .
REX:	Do I wear the gat in this scene?
REGGIE:	Yes, you do, Rex, but you don't use it. Just put the gat in your pocket . . .
NICK:	(INTERIOR) I could think of a place where the sun didn't shine where I'd like to put that gat up. But,

for the first time in my life, I was working for myself, whoever that was. If you believed what you heard over the radio, I was a guy with a sewer-pipe voice and a taste for tea. On the covers of the pulps, my meaty hands ripped the dresses off palpitating quails. In the movies I was strictly for wimps.

REX: Reggie, do I wear the hat in this scene?

REGGIE: Not that one, it doesn't match. Where's that damn stunt double? Boy, give me your hat!

NICK: Huh? Sure, here.

REGGIE: This one, Rex.

REX: Now, Reggie. Where is this scene in the damn story? Have I been to Hell City already? Or did I just hear the Reverend on the radio?

REGGIE: Well, I don't know . . .

NICK: (INTERIOR, LOOKING AT THE HAT HE'S BEEN GIVEN) Jesus, look at this! If it wasn't a clue, it might as well be one — an octopus in a hat! Or at least a picture of one. Why hadn't I see it before? So that Radio Reverend and his crazy cultists were involved.

REGGIE: (TO NICK) You, boy. What's your name?

NICK: Ah — Ding. I call myself Bill Ding.

REGGIE: Alright, boy. Just show us the fall you just took again.

NICK: But why do you . . .

REGGIE: C'mon, c'mon! You're shot — bang, bang, bang, bang, bang, bang! And you fall!

NICK TAKES ANOTHER DIVE

REGGIE: There, did you see, Rex?

REX:	Yes, beautiful . . . but really, Reggie, this line — do you think a real American detective would say, "The world was spinning like an owl in a strait-jacket tailored for a trip to Hell?" I mean — wouldn't he just moan and fall over just like he did?
NICK:	You said it, Brother.
REGGIE:	Aha! That's the rewrite. Let's go back to the pink pages . . . See! (READING) "The world was spinning like a fork in life's sordid sewer." Much better.
REX:	Can you say "fork" in American films?
REGGIE:	You can call it a damn "prong" if you want.
REX:	How about "squid-sticker"?
REGGIE:	That's fine . . .
NICK:	(INTERIOR) It was time to sit down on brass tacks. I had to make a move. I was gonna ask 'em to forget about frog-stickers or squid-stickers . . . it was time to throw something else into the hat — an octopus!
REGGIE:	What did you say?
NICK:	I said — let's try an octopus in a hat! Look at this!
REGGIE:	My God! Who are you?
REX:	Yes, just who do you think you are?
NICK:	I'm you, buddy-boy! I'm — the real Nick Danger!
ARCHIE:	Hold it right there!

ARCHIE SLUGS NICK FROM BEHIND AND NICK FALLS FACE DOWN TO THE FLOOR.

BIG MUSIC CHORD SUSTAINS AS THE SCENE BLACKS OUT.

BEN BLAND RETURNS TO THE SCREEN. HE SEEMS TO BE SNOOZING.

VOICE OF HIS PRODUCER: Ben!

BEN: Oh, ah, yes. I'm back — all day all night — back to the All Day All Night Movie Matinee Marathon. We're gonna have some photos of the orphans the mercenary sold, later on, and . . . I guess there's no winner on our Nostalgia Quiz today. So there's the answer on your screen. Quite a surprise, huh? And that means another five dollar Gibberson quarter-plump half-roasted owl in the Trivia Pot. Now this:

SHIFTER: I'm not a doctor, and I've never even been to one, but this is going by so fast that you probably think I am a doctor — and that's why I'm being well-paid to introduce you to my Dr. Shifter's Stop & Start Clinics. You say you want to stop smoking and start driving? Stop over-eating and start drinking? Or do you want to start exercising, stop bedwetting and give speed-reading up for good? Well, now you can have the choice — and you can do it all under one roof — your own! Because when you sign up, you turn your home into another local neighborhood Dr. Shifter's Stop & Start Clinic. Big flashing sign and 150-foot extension cord cheerfully included.

Free demonstration today and tomorrow — just look for the big flashing sign on your neighbor's lawn. Dr. Shifter's Stop & Start Clinics Franchise Inc. Today at the home of Joey Demographico, 1333-and-a-third Air Freshener Blvd., Terra Linda, California. Stop whatever you're doing and start one today!

PRODUCER: Ben!

BEN: Time for the movie! I'll just feed the fishies and get into my bed and I bet you will too. So back to "Men In Hats."

WHEN WE RETURN, NICK IS DRIVING

NICK: (INTERIOR) I drove out on one of those roads with a Spanish name that drift up into one of those canyons that crease the edge of one of those towns called

Los Angeles. I was just another guy in a hat looking for a murderer on a rainy night.

HE BARELY MISSES A SWERVING CAR

NICK: Look out! Must be some tourist from Ohio looking for that little orange ranch of his dreams! Fat chance! Only the rich live this high. Like poor old Rex Spoffard — very high, very rich, and very dead . . .

FLASHBACK . . .

REX: (ON PHONE) You've got to listen to me, Danger . . .

NICK: It was his nickel.

REX: I know you are who you think you are — and somebody else knows I think so too. You see — it was me in that little film. Oh, I had on hip boots and an owl mask, but it was me — me! And my dog. And my daughter! He's trying to ruin me. His tentacles are everywhere. You've got to help me! Help . . . help . . . ehhhhh . . .

NICK: Someone sure helped him — helped themselves to his life. It was getting darker and wetter. I poured another two fingers out of the glove compartment . . .

FLASHBACK . . .

PEGGY: Pour one for me too, Nick. Only make it a double. One for hello and one for goodbye. I don't need you anymore, Nick! If I wanna see you, I can see you in the movies. I can read you in bed between soft, hot covers. Everybody owns you now, Nick! You don't own yourself! You're a Dick With No Name — and you better not go looking for it or you'll lose your life! . . . life . . . life . . .

NICK IS STILL DRIVING

NICK: Poor dead Peggy, if that was her name. She had tried to level with me — but now she's on a slab with a tag around her big toe — a tag that reads "Nancy." . . . The road was rough and turned to dirt at the top of the ridge. That was OK with me. I was beginning to like dirt. Felt right at home.

FLASHBACK...

BRADSHAW: Get your nose out of the quicksand, Danger! Or I'll dust you off! All you got is a picture of a squid in a lid and a receipt for fifteen thousand dollars worth of murder from the Radio Reverend up at Hell City. I'm passing. I've got two stiffs in the cooler with your name on their lips — so get lost, soldier. Don't bother me. Get lost... lost... lost...

NICK: Was I lost? There were no directions!

HE BRINGS THE CAR TO A SCREECHING HALT

NICK: Jesus, a dead end! I was anywhere but lost. Looming out of the dark were the gates to Hell City. I could tell by the dim sign — an eight-legged neon friend of mine in a fedora.

NICK GETS OUT OF HIS CAR

NICK: It was dark. No moon. Lonely owls hooting. It was strictly a night for a warm, crackling fire and a bosomy doll.

ROCKY APPEARS WITH A FLASHLIGHT ON NICK

NICK: What was that?

NICK TURNS HIS FLASHLIGHT ON ROCKY

ROCKY: Good evening... Mr. Danger!

NICK: Rococo, you wheezing sleazle! Some things never change!

ROCKY: I've got you covered, Danger. I've got a gun, see?

NICK: Yeah? Well, I've got one too.

BOTH AT ONCE: So there you are! Don't move!

THEY CIRCLE EACH OTHER, WITH LIGHTS ON THEIR FACES.

FRED MAY, THE IMMORTAL PITCHMAN, APPEARS

FRED: Are these the kind of men you'd like to be caught out at night with? If the answer is "no," let Detective Dating Service go to work for you! Now, here's an attractive young man — he says he's thirty years old, makes over thirty thousand a year in unreported income, always seems to have cocaine and is looking for girls who love other girls. And we've found her! She says she's twenty-two, wears edible underwear and loves TVs. Though she claims she started "dating" at sixteen — we've got film on her at eleven!! So whether you like Girls, Guys, Dogs or Bi's, you'll be surprised when you give the case to Detective Dating Service!

LIGHTS OUT AND CURTAIN

The tribute to Fred May left Ben Bland alone in the studio, awaiting his return "next time" on the Matinee. And Ben would be blearily back to host another Danger movie in "Joey's House."

(This logo does not signify an endorsement!)

Firesign with Larry Josephson at Airlie III

CHAPTER 4
THE HISTORY OF THE ART OF RADIO

It was a gray, wet April. The Roxy gig had happened. I bought a car — a new, blue 1979 Datsun 310. Great car. A few days went by.

April 2nd — Had to call PA on Sun — concerned abt the situation — wanted to let him know I wasn't hiding off on a "vacation" but that I was ready to work & feel that writing is very important. Maybe it was just paranoia, but I felt the situation slipping. PA had been working on PB — convinced him that our movie was really "Men In Hats" & sold him on "our" story — whatever that ultimately turns out to be.

April 4th — Today things began to seem like the long silent Spring days of the past 5 years. A depression coming on this week, sparked prob by the end of the show, subsequent exhaustion and realization that TFT only exists when it is working. . . Spoke to a dour PA last night — no light anywhere it wld seem. HBO now seems dead, w/P&B only involved for themselves. PA wants to get a treatment in order for Avco/Embassy. Talking abt "O&O show" as basis for movie — this to take adv of Joey char for PB, I guess.

Apr 11th — A mocker singing. Cloudy late eve — canyon dark at PB's . . . So it's been all talk. Resolved ND identity/Firesign identity question by getting PP's active contribution to having TFT play ND — still leaving room for the "guest star." An agreement to the way we will appear AS TFT. Also agreement on period film plus strangenesses. I feel satisfied. Also much talk abt contract — which is close to signing, really.

Danger was all ours, really. And certainly all Phil's. Noir comedy come to life as we argue about Nick's identity. What IS Reality? Sure, the Guest Star can be a name and we'll have fun around him. Driving in the Compromise Lane on the Hollywood Freeway.

Then a discussion of the 5-nite a week TV series — pinning down an identity for it — TFT looks at _____ — some diff and unpredictable topic each nite, easy-going format allowing improv.

An unexpected invitation came from radio producer Larry Josephson (he brought back the immortal Bob & Ray for my NPR "Sunday Show" a few years later) for Firesign to appear at the awesomely titled "1979 Corporation For Public Broadcasting Radio Development Workshops" later that month at a rural enclave called Airlie, in Virginia. We were to perform "something" on Sunday and participate, if we wanted to, in the workshops, which were largely about fund-raising. Austin, who hadn't flown to a Firesign event in five years or so, would come in by phone-line. That seemed fine — it was radio, wasn't it?

Fri noon — S[anta]B[arbara]. A beautiful spring day — succulents and pyrocantha in bloom and bees everywhere. Got home abt 6 yest after work day at Peter's — we finished the Airlie piece and outlined a proposal for the Movietone News. A good day's work, all going along well. Wed we wrote the Airlie show pt. 1 & then took a mtg w/Jennifer Gladstone on a Goldwyn proposal for a 5-nite-a-week 11pm comedy show pilot.

Geeze, maybe for five minutes. I can't imagine how we would've handled five nights a week! It was a product of a fevered imagination.

Along with the new material for Airlie, we included some bits from our 1969 "single," "Forward Into The Past," and a version (one of many) of "The American Pageant" from our second album. The piece would end with a nod to our early public radio fund-raising gigs at Pacifica stations.

Sunday Apr 22 — Airlie VA — 8 am
In Bldg 41, the loudest sound you can hear is the ticking of the big ol' wall clock. Also the birds — a continuous rhapsody of songs, chirps & honks dominating the rolling countryside. The motto of Airlie is "All For the Best." There's a bust of Melvin Laird in the room we're appearing in. Rumor has it that the CIA keeps Russian defectors in a remote Safe House on these acres. No phones & no TVs in Bldg 41 — but very plush carpet & furniture that no Tropicana vandals will ever get a hold of.

Tues Apr 24 — Noon
Birds are still chattering like a primeval woods. Goose honks. It's a wet am — misty and Springlike. Today have had b'fast at 8 and attended seminar on ratings already. Seemed a subject on which there was & only could be grudging agreement & (or) hopeless disagreement. . . . Drama "wkshop" followed w/ J. Houseman. I thot he was a bit superfluous, if a sentimental touchstone. Wkshop a disappointment. Richard Imison was well-spoken but no one really had a lot to say — and there were very few people there.

Sun — a long quiet am w/a couple of pleasant walks. We moved over to The Silo House in the aft — a much more motley affair w/a pool & the bar. Ate, socialized

& got ready for the show. PA's transmission was marred only by the phone line into Airlie — he really sounded fine. Altho I thot the piece had its ups & downs & wasn't sure how it went over, we did get an enthusiastic response & even a partial standing "ovation."

It was largely inspired by the many collections of "historic broadcasts," on LP and especially one that featured just the openings of one old show after another. We eventually called the piece "The History of the Art of Radio" and performed it in various editions thereafter. Here's how it went.

THE HISTORY OF THE ART OF RADIO OR, Everything You Know About Wradio is Rong

PB:	The problem is — people here are losing touch with the reason for this convention.
PP:	That's right. How can you get other people to listen to the radio when they aren't listening to the radio themselves?
DO:	So get off the podium, Josephson, turn off the lights and we'll turn on the radio . . .
PP:	Tonight The Firesign Theatre is here to prove, once and for all, that . . .
PA:	(AS HARRY COX, COMING IN BY SATELLITE) Everything You Know Is Wrong — about the History of the Art of Radio-o-o-o-o-o . . .
DO:	Amazing! What you have just heard is the voice of Professor Harry Cox, thrown by satellite halfway across the world from his giant communications center at Space 11, in the Blue Mouse Trailer Retirement Camp at Hellmouth, California. Harry — are you there?
HARRY:	How're ya doin, boys?
PB:	How's it look from there, Harry?
HARRY:	From where?

PB: From there in the trailer court.

HARRY: I'm not in the trailer court. I'm on the satellite. Some kind of a mistake. I'm holdin' on for dear life!

PP: How high are you, Harry?

HARRY: How high are you? But seriously, I don't suppose that most people down there know that inane wireless communications like this have been going on since the dawn of rewritten history.

PB: According to our most recently approved schoolbooks we've been told that wireless transmission was invented by General Spaghetini "The Clicker" Mecchoroni in the little town of Piso-Electrico.

HARRY: Yes! No! Not so! According to Dr. Peter Savatte of the Carlos Sagan-Von Daniken Institute of Copies Available In The Lobby. Dr. Savatte?

PP (AS SAVATTE, TERRIBLE ACCENT): Thank you.

EVERYBODY ELSE: You're welcome.

SAVATTE: In my latest book, "Hubcaps of the Gods," available in drugstores everywhere, I have just conclusively demonstrated that the first truly wireless civilization was the ancient Druids of India. I personally oversaw a secret excavation team that investigated the hitherto inexplicable discovery of hundreds of mounds of dry batteries, which have been rusting in relative silence for over two hundred thousand years, in a mysteriously arid region of the vast Plain of Beljarrs, near Plath, outside Calcutta, like nearly everything else in India. Amidst the myriad artifacts uncovered — replicas of which, by the way, are available as you leave the lobby, ancient batteries not included — our excavating team found not one scrap, not one trace, one shred or one fragment — of wires! Thus proving incontraclusively that prehistoric Druidic India was — the first Wireless Society. Thank me and I'm welcome.

| PB: | How ironic that this secret, like so many other ancient secrets, should be delayed for centuries, like a check in the mail, forcing in the interim, the invention of — wire! |

VOICES MURMURING UNDER

| DO: | (AS REPORTER) We're here, it's July 12th, 1843 — another insufferable, swampy day in the stuffy Supreme Court chambers in Washington D.C. and — "We Are Here!" And why are we here? Exactly! Wire. Why, we are awaiting the first transmission from Baltimore, Maryland, by the talented fingers of Samuel F. B. Morose — an inventor so poor that he has to wait until Night Rates Apply before he sends his historic First Message! |

| PB: | (AS JUSTICE) Gentlemen, your attention, please! I believe it's now 6 o'clock and the message should be coming through. |

| PA: | (VIA SATELLITE) Dit dit, dah dit, dah dah dit, dit dit dit, dah dah dit! |

VOICES HUZZAH AND APPLAUSE

| DO: | (AS COUNTRY CHARACTER) By cracky, Mr. Cheap Justice, sir! That come thru clear as a belljar! |

| JUSTICE: | What does it say? |

| PP: | It says "Dit dit, dah dit, dah dah dit, dit dit dit, dah dah dit!" |

VOICES MORE HUZZAHS AND APPLAUSE

| REPORTER: | That's truly amazing. Excuse me, Mr. Cheap Justice? Could you perhaps interpret this message further for us? |

| JUSTICE: | Of course I could. That's my job. I spend whole sweaty days interpreting pieces of paper. Let's see . . . I think it's in some sort of street slang — a meaty

	patois, a belle jargon. Dash it all! This is tough! I'll just have to say — it's about dis and dot.
DO:	It was indeed about dis and dot — and just what did dis dot wrought?
PA:	(SATELLITE) It wrought the call of Progress!
SFX:	PHONE RING AND PICKUP
PP:	(AS BELLJAR) Hello? Alexander Grahamcrackerbox Belljar here — inventor of the phone company. It's Mr. Watson, I presume. What can I do for you?
PA:	(AS WATSON) I've stumbled across the most frightful conspiracy! A plot to ensnare the world in wires and poles! To fill the homes of the poor with ringing noises! To allow men to talk to naked women without their knowing it! And worst of all — to charge great sums of money, while cutting off service to pathetic old people who then freeze to death in their homes! Holmes! Do you hear me, Holmes?
PP:	Ah-hem. I'm horrendously sorry, old fellow, but you've got the wrong number.
SFX:	DISCONNECT AND DIAL TONE

VOICES TALK TO ONE ANOTHER UNDER

DO:	(BRIT) While people all over the world paired up to talk to one another, the brilliant German scientist Heinrich Megaherz, alone on his own in 'is 'ome in Cologne, was sniffing the all-pervasive ether and immediately had a vision. A strange vision of electric waves undulating relentlessly along limpid, invisible molecular highways of oscillating, shimmering electromagnetic fields. He also saw dragons, little guys in melty hats and the last three episodes of "Time Out for Beaver."
PB:	Soon, news of his discovery spread far and wide and, on America's East Coast, the image of surfing on undulating electromagnetic waves had a particular

	appeal to a bored, sandy-haired young college student at Yale named Tree de Forrest, and would lead him eventually to really clean up, when he invented the Vacuum Cleaner!
PP:	(OFF) No, Pete. Tube. The vacuum tube!
PB:	I mean, the vacuum tube. Or was it the vacuum-tube-powered vacuum cleaner? Well, anyway — he knew what it was and what to do with it!
DO:	And not a moment too soon, because we needed it to light up a sign that said:
PP:	"On The Air!"
SFX:	STATIC UNDER
PB:	(AS LANE) Hello, America. This is Jackson Lane, the honeysweet voice of station KWKW in Vasoline, New Jersey.
SFX:	BURST OF STATIC
LANE:	From our modern studio one full floor above Ray's Hardware at the busy intersection of Darwin and Sumac, we bring you the tender tenor tones of Lurch Murphy and the Boys of County Beljar!
PP:	(SINGING, WITH 78 RECORD SURFACE NOISE) When Irish eyes are smilin' Sure 'tis like a balmy day! And when Irish bombs are blastin' It'll blow the pub away-tik-away-tik-away-tik-away— (NEEDLE LIFTED) ziiiip!
DO:	So, America was on the air! There was only one problem with being on the air. Once you're on, you have to stay on, and on, and on, and on—ziiiip! Hour after hour, day after day, week after week, month after month, year after year, decade after . . .
ALL:	Dave! C'mon, Dave . . .

DO:	Well, you get the point. And all of it was lies!
ALL:	Dave!!!
DO:	Live! I meant "Live!"
PB:	1932. The White House.
PP:	You're on, Mr. President.
FDR:	My fellow Americans. Before I read to you from the funny papers, our daily rendez-vous with Disney, let me first make one thing perfectly clear — all we have to fear — is me . . .
PB:	1934. The Pissgarten Olympic Auditorium in Horsetapple, Bavaria. The scene of the broadcast of the Schmelling-Herring fight.
PP:	(STATIC UNDER) I'm in the back of this giant auditorium, where the great big white man and the great big black man are trading a tremendous series of punches! From where I'm sitting, it's a lot easier to see the great big white man than the great big black man — and now — now the white man is slowly turning red, illuminated by the flickering, almost hypnotic glow of the torches, as he is being pummelled by the great big black man's smoking hamlike fists.
ALL:	CROWD ROARS
PP:	And Herring's down! The white man is down! And the Germans are up! They're dressed in brown, very easy to see, as they rush to the fallen Herring's aid. And now, they are embracing the big black man in a kind of a "beer hug" and hoisting him around the ring now, lifting him higher, with the roars of approval ringing from the crowd, lifting him higher now and — throwing him out of ring! And now, they're propping up the comatose form of the bleeding white man, pulling up his arm — and it looks like the red Herring has been declared the unconscious New World's Champion! What an upset!!

PB:	1937. Lakehurts, New Jersey. The Naval Gasbag Landing Field.
SFX:	WIND
PA:	(BY SATELLITE) I can see the great ship Hindenburg now, the majestic hulk, hovering over the mooring pylon. There's still a hint of rain in the air. Oh, oh, the wind seems to be coming up a bit, there. There's the ground crew, like ants, running out to man the ropes. The huge ship is only about a hundred feet overhead. I can see tiny people waving through the windows — wait a minute! My God! The ship is heeling over to the left! A big gust of wind, and — there's a spark, there! And — it rights itself. It's come around. The last of the ropes is being secured . . . and here come the passengers, a few of them goose-stepping to get the circulation back in their legs after the long trans-Atlantic flight. There's Happy Chandler! There's Judge Crater! . . . And that's the story here from Lakehurts . . .
DO:	Yes, the news may have kept America wired to their seats, but it was the Art of Radio that really glued 'em to their sets!
PB:	Is it a hit?
SFX:	SOCK!
PB:	Or a miss?
PP:	(GIRL) What?
APPLAUSE	
PB:	Yes, yes, yes! The makers of Loose Blood present The Aboriginal Amateur Hour! And here's your menial host, Major Arcana!
SFX:	RATCHET
PP:	Round and round I go. Hey, hey, babe! We're on the wheel again! But first, here's a word for you sufferers

	from Blood Sludge from the wealthy folks at Driml . . .
MUSIC:	CHORD, HUMMING UNDER
PA:	End of So . . . !
DO:	The timeless story of the Little People, striving to make a piepond of tranquility in a dirty, back-stabbing, self-righteous hamlet that accepts neither, but rejects both. Brought to you every day by Bree!
ALL:	Bree! Bree! Bree! Clean! Clean! Clean!
PB:	"Cleaner Than Anything!"
PP:	HUMMING UNDER
DO:	As you remember, Cookie, ejected from Dr. Dogg's Insane Asylum, had just been driven out to the scene of the fire in Aubrey's stolen car. Only a few minutes before, the carrots and the squirrels had formed a committee to flood the Mixville Breadworks before nightfall, and, in court, Nora voids to unlock the pent-up riddle of Blessed Father Earpo, before we all reach — the End of Song . . .
DO:	DIT DIT DITS
PA:	Headquarters. Headquarters. Moon 40 Taurus.
PB:	Roger!
PA:	Sun 29 Pisces.
PB:	Roger! Roger?
DO:	What?
PB:	This one looks serious, Roger. Cancer is rising!
DO:	Then we'd better call — Cap-tain Equinox!!!!
PP:	Captain Equinox! The deadliest foe of those who would test our Island democracy! By day, Adolf

	Tree — a mild-mannered college professor. By night — Kiki! A mini-skirted habitué of Hollywood's star-struck Sunset Strip. But twice a year he's . . .
DO:	Cap-tain Equinox!!!!
PB:	Today's dumb story, "Spies Over Broadway," but first . . .
PA:	(MANIC LAUGH) Don't Crush That Dwarf! Come in! I'm the Strange Dr. Weird, and you've just entered the Vault of Mindless Fellowship!!! (LAUGHS)
PP:	Police State!
PB:	Police State!
DO:	Police State!
PB:	Help! It's the Police!
PP:	(SINGS) Policemen, real Policemen! It's Policemen we'll become!
DO/PB:	Who's Number One?
PP:	(SINGS) Peace Men! Yes, we're Peace Men! Even though we wear a gun!
DO/PB:	It's all in fun!
PP:	HUMS UNDER
PB:	Police State! Where green rookies become hardened men in blue. Where Danger earns a diploma and Crime gets taught the lesson it deserves! Listen now as the Federal Bureau of Marijuana, in cooperation with Crime Lord Magazine, presents Challenge Number 13 — "Roach Patrol!" — at Police State!
DO:	(LAUGHING) Do pigs live in trees?
SFX:	TICK-TOCK, HONK, BUZZER

DO: (GIRL) What?

PP: (SINGS) If you lived where I live
 And you lived where you lived
 Then we'd live where pigs live —
 In trees . . .
 Yes, yes, we all live in trees — like pigs!

APPLAUSE

PB: And it's time again to play . . .

DO: (GIRL) What?

PB: The all-family fun game that stunts the experts!

PA: The Whispering Yeast Hour. With the Whispering Yeast Symphonette, the famous Whispering Yeast All-Animal Whistling Choir, and yours truly, Dwight Yeast. And now, our musical director, Father Earpo Saweeny joins the Whispering Yeast All-Animal Whistling Choir in a rousing Salute To Reality!

WHISTLING, ANIMALS

DO: Such was the state of the Art of Radio back there in the 1930s — or was it just the art of selling soap and cigarettes to a gullible American Public? Well, we can thank our Lucky Strikes — uh, Stars — for thoughtful, concerned dramatists — the poets of the medium. Big men, like Awesome Welles, who scared the pants off us, and thin men, like William Powell, who didn't. But perhaps the greatest producer of them all was the man who transformed our Great American Art of Selling into the Art of Selling Us A Greater America. I'm speaking, of course, of radio dramatist Normal Corny — er, Corwin, who yanked radio into the 1940s by the ears. Here is his most influential broadcast, first heard December 6th, 1940 on the Red, White and Blue Networks — his immortal classic, "Who Am Us Anyway?"

A version of "The American Pageant"
was inserted into the show here.

*Check it out in the 8 Shoes version
a bit later in the book.*

DO: So we went to the Wars. And when we came back we discovered another casualty rather close to home — it was radio. We found that suddenly we couldn't hear De Forrest for the bees. You see, a swarm of bees had buzzed in a vision through Philo Farnsworth's head and had led him to invent the cathode ray tube! But then, it was the Fifties, and B's were everywhere — B-movies, B-girls . . .

PP: (SINGING) "Be my love, for no one else can end this yearning . . .

DO: And "Time Out For Beaver." America was bewitched by television and nobody seemed very bothered at being bewildered! And radio was left to the kids, locked tight in their rooms, late at night, under covers, blanketed in secrecy, listening to . . .

PA/PP: ROCK 'N' ROLL SONG UNDER

PB: Hello, Detroit, Cleveland, Philadelphia, Fresno, Denver and all you sweet people at the Fall Ball — what they call the Spring Fling — at Tacoma High. Whatever it is! And say! It's here! R & B and Beer! I'm talkin' bout Cleveland's own — lucky Here Beer. I drink it, because it's Here! So, if you're of age, drink Here! And if you ain't there yet, then drink Near Here! That's Here Beer! Let's hear it! Now, the next tune is goin' out to Little Larry J, Nancy, Tiny Hitler, the Wounded Man, and ever'body down there — and I do mean "down" — at the corner of 199th and Froggman in Detroit, Cleveland, Philadelphia and (FADING) Fresno, Denver . . .

DO: With that dedication ringing in our ears we listened to the AM in the a.m. and the p.m. and then along came FM and h-fi and WBAI . . . This is WBAI, 99.5 in New York City. And you've just heard William Malloch's Bowel Movement in B-minus, performed by the — unpronounceable Wind Symphony Orchestra, under the superb direction of — ah, Sir Muffled

	Foreign-Name! And this concludes the two hours we have been able to keep the transmitter on today. Now, sty to tay stuned as long as you can, as we present the transcribed BBC classic, "The Ring of the Orphan King."
SFX:	WIND
PP:	(AS EGMONT) I see him not, the ghost of my dead stepfather. And yet, the soldiers swear, while King Alphonso's blessed body lies below, his vexed spirit stalks above in King-sized sheets. They tell me to beware. Must I obey? As a tiny tot my frosty foster mother told me not to cross the moat. And then, the monk he did bespeak me "cast the moat from mine own eye." And so, confused, I crossed mine eyes and double-crossed the monk, who fell into the moat! Then, soon, my naughty nubile niece, Marie, did bid me warning that I play no longer by myself — 'twould make me blind to her entreaties; and so I leapt into her burning bush, and lo, although consumed with fire, I rose again to bite another apple on yet another Eve. Are we not men? If we fall, can we not but rise again? Hot-headed, flush'd with blood — we'll not take it lying down! We'll prop it up and get it any way we can! Oh, listeners! Save me! . . .
PB:	Yes, you can help to save us, here at KPFK, Los Angeles, dear listeners. It's Marathon time again and we only have six thousand dollars of our sixty thousand dollar goal and Elliot Mintz has fallen asleep, and Austin and Ossman and Paul Dallas are all mad at me because of that Corvette offer I made this morning and I promise I'll get back to the Tarot card readings in a minute, but first, you people've got to start calling in with subscriptions or I swear I'm going back to Germany to finish my art film.
DO:	(TOKING) Listen, Peter, there's a phone call coming on.
PB:	Oh, good . . . KPFK Marathon. You're on the air.

PA: (BY SATELLITE, AS HARRY COX) Mr. Bergman? This is the Hanged Man. What is a horse-leech? Whatever happened to Mel Noel? No, seriously, I do believe in flying saucers because I found out long ago that "Everything We Know Is Wrong!"

PB: Oh, no, it's Harry Cox again.

DO: Listen, Harry, we're not talking about "everything" tonight, we're just talking about the History of Fund Raising on Listener-Sponsored Radio.

PA: Oh.

PP: That's right, Dave. And that really lies in the hands of the jet-lagged, foundation-fed delegates right here in this room.

DO: That's right, Phil. It's in their heads now.

ALL: So good luck and good night . . .

CHAPTER 5
FROM BRECHT, VIA WILLIE THE SHAKE, TO JOEY'S HOUSE WE GO

The offer to appear at the Ojai Music Festival on May 20th 1979 came from Bill Malloch, a dear friend, once Music Director at KPFK, a record collector, musicologist, composer and producer. We were invited to portray Clowns in the cast of "The Lesson," with a text by Bertold Brecht and music by Paul Hindemith. The piece was about a pilot who calls upon his fellow men for help when his plane crashes.

We Clowns had our own grim scene, "Do Men Help Each Other?" in which we cure a giant of his afflictions by sawing off his affected limbs, one by one. The scene caused a scandal (which pleased Herr Brecht, though it was wordless) at the premiere in 1929. Firesign got paid $500 for our debut in musical mime. The eminent Lukas Foss conducted and Werner Klemperer (of "Hogan's Heros" fame) narrated. The Fighting Clowns were born on a sunny outdoor stage in a little town behind LA's back.

This was the Ojai Festival weekend — we took Alla Rakha out there Sat am & stayed for the "east meets east" concert with R. Shankar — the 60s revisited. It was all very pleasant. . . . Sun we went back to Ojai . . . We did our rehearsal first — PB was down about things & everyone was a bit distant — but all was well. PB brought his girlfriend — no great beauty, but nice. PP alone and a bit lonely looking. PA arr. late, but in good spirits. The concert itself was a real hit — our 10 mins was a hi-lite certainly & by the time we did it we were into our "Schmidt Brothers" characters . . .

A couple of classy dates, and we had proof we could pipe Austin in if we had to. Here's the music for our Scene For Clowns:

Firesign in the Studio with Shakespeare, 1980

I'd been in touch with a number of National Public Radio producers over the past few months, negotiating for spots on "All Things Considered," and the brand-new "Morning Edition." Public radio's long-running drama series, "earplay," had bought a script of mine, based on the work of e. e. cummings and were in the midst of a production of it when I suggested that Firesign contribute to their next (and final, as it turned out) season.

At our next meeting after Clowning at Ojai we talked about an "earplay" production of a fully re-written version of "Anythynge You Want To," our endlessly evolving take on Shakespeare and all things "thea-tuh." The decision was to go with a "record album-style" studio production. We made another Roxy date for July 26-28 and continued our regular sketches for NPR.

Thurs aft — May 24 — PB's
Today we wrote AYWT new Act 1, sc. 1 — the Cooks on the heath. Good work. Yest we put in an hour on 3 radio pieces for NPR & then wrote the Prolog — which was hard. Recorded in Hollywood in the evening — went very well after a slow start — insistence on improv'ing the pieces paid off in two very funny bits. Glad to break the P&B-style hold on having to write everything — the looseness really shows. Doesn't sound like other comedy groups or commercials.

On Tues we listened to records, talked the project & worked out a scene-structure that satisfied everyone. I like the symmetry of it — very much more Shakespearian.

Mon 4 June 79 — am
Going back to last week's work in LA — drove in Tuesday & worked at PP's — mostly re-writing "shipwreck-Tempest" scene and had a good time. Wed we rewrote "Ghost" scene — our least inspired day, but OK still. Thur we got onto a new scene — 2 new ones really in a new Act 2 — fisherman and Bishop — had a great time with them — continued working at PP's — lots of coffee & grub. Very good working relations.

Sunday, June 10 — pm
Thurs and Fri in LA — very hard as the work took a difficult turn half way thru. We were really stuck on Thurs & very argumentative & short of temper. Wrote on Fri — opening and 1st interval, a gravedigger scene to precede short Ed/Marie scene. Finished that & went on to begin Ed Ed/Nuncle scene — worked to the bitter end of the day — 7:30. PB depressed after an eventful trip "home" to Mendo — really identifying w/it, voting in the special election, etc. PA feisty & in one of those moods where I can't satisfy him. I was down too — worried abt piece being too trivial & "special."

Wed — June 13
Mon — drove in — heat really bad in SF Valley — traffic slow & car hot. Met at PP's which is pleasant — wrote the missing "Count" scene in Act 2 so, with a few touches, the Act was finished.

Slept OK & got up & out by 9 am — drove to Laurel Can & Ventura & ate b'fast at Tiny Naylor's & had the Datsun washed and gassed up (it was an even day) at the station next door. All very efficient. Then went on to PB's, smoked a j & went on to our mtg at PP's.

We had considerable discussion on the direction & content of the 3rd Act, then wrote the 2nd interval and began the 1st scene — did pretty well at it by day's end.

Events speed up toward studio time.

14 June — Thurs eve
Balmy & loud w/birds. Well, next to last day and only one scene to do — work stretches out to fit the time available to it.

Yest never really got started — lots of P&B business that kept them on the phone until mid-afternoon. Wrote the ending of 3.1 at the end of aft & discussed the remainder of the act. I stayed for chili w/Philly and then we went to see "China Syndrome" which I pretty much liked.

Another pretty hard-fought day — very close attention to the writing and everyone alternately holding out for something. But we got the 2 war scenes we'd discussed & that put us at the end. So tomorrow we expect to wrap it up.

PB is pretty much burned out w/it, I'd say. PP is also tired of it all. Even PA was silent today, but fought hard for Edmund's blood-lust. It really IS an unusual collaboration. Four writers are a lot to please.

Tonight we're going out to eat, then record for NPR. Tomorrow will be a rigorous one — one that's been bought & must be paid for.

Tues — 19 June — "The Street"
Pleasant am in BH. About to begin day 2 of production on AYWT. I drove in very early yest & we had a long day at the studio. Got abt 40% of the voice tracks recorded — much more than we had expected, & we were off to a slow start. Moods were OK, workmanlike. The material sounds good — maybe too good & not funny enough. Donno. Some SFX & music will help. I'm only concerned we won't be too long.

Wed am — 27 June 79 — PP's place
The past week has gone by w/such a level of activity that I haven't been able to get any of it down & it's all been fascinating.

We continued our production thru last week in the studio — voice tracks on Tues, Diz White's scenes on Wed, effects and overdubbing Thurs & Fri. All fit together very well — very long studio days — until 7:30 pm.

Yest — up early and pack the car & into LA. Recorded the music tracks most of the day, then some SFX. After, we went out w/Larry Josephson to the Brown Derby for a $200 dinner. PP was fairly outrageous & we all had a good time.

The wonderful English comedy writer and actress, Diz White, of "Bullshot Crummond" fame, gave us a memorable Marie and Ben Wright, "Your Host," London-born radio ("Sherlock Holmes"), film and voice actor, was our link with the "BBC."

Sunday am — July 1st
A warm & beautiful summer day — light breeze blowing. The past week in LA was the smoggiest in years — fortunately I was in the air-conditioned studio, so it didn't bother me too much.

We finished AYWT last Friday at 9 pm — just half a day long. Production was a bit rushed — but I don't think anyone will notice. The work on Wed included recording Ben Wright. We just got a start on mastering on Thurs eve & finished Fri. A glitch here & there — we had to rerecord 2 lines that had been accidentally erased. Playback on Fri night pleased us all — champ. toasts to the future & much excitement. It really is a major feat — 1st audio work in 5 years — together w/MIHats, a great beginning to FSII.

Lost hearing partially in my right ear last Wed — still plaguing me & I'll have to see the Doc tomorrow.

Friday noon — 6 July
Monday I called the ear Dr. in the am & went in the late aft. Got examined ($70 worth) & really ended up not knowing much — "traumatic hearing loss" — put on a diet of low salt, no caffeine & niacin to make the blood rush in my ears I guess.

Yest I had a downer day — depressed. Maybe all the excitement of production gone — feeling of non-achievement for all the work. Thought of Steve Martin in a million & a half house in Montecito — well!

Steve Martin had appeared with us at our first club date in early 1968. He played the banjo, made balloon animals and cracked some jokes. Nice guy. Passed us on the left going top speed. I may have been a bit envious.

Friday am — 20 July
End of the week — one more day of new writing today, then a dinner party at PA's tonite & home for the weekend. Mon — drove in to town during the heat — scorching in the valley. Photo session went very well — pix look great — but heat was terrific — drank beer & smoked j's and bulled thru 5 or 6 different set-ups — still hot when we finished.

Tues — worked on revising the O&O script all day. Wed we cut & revised & talked Nick Danger. Thurs we finally got down to writing — 1st ND scene & half the 2nd. We are really down to it now — 3 days of rehearsal next week & then Roxy weekend. The new show is still very hazy. It's simplified alright — the "news" is gone from it — less exhausting for sure. Is it a long way from the show we opened? Or is the essence of it unchanged?

It was an entirely new Nick Danger we wrote for "Joey's House." The mirror-maze-movie that we'd designed to fit into the general Hellscape of our first draft was chucked. Too complicated. We'd also created an intentionally profane prime-time sit-com, "Thank You, Mr. President," as a stand-alone sketch. It cropped up here and there when needed and was still in the 1981 touring show. That script appears later in this book. Much of the scripted dialog for "Joey's House" is improv-free and reads a little spare on the page. Each performance of the show was driven by Firesign's impulse to mock the script, talk to the audience, try to trip one another up and generally to re-write the jokes off-stage without waiting for intermission.

Triptych of the three bills advertising Firesign at the Roxy.

Snapshot, Firesign at home circa May 1979.

JOEY'S HOUSE

THE CHARACTERS:

PHIL AUSTIN played   MOM (MADGE) DEMOGRAPHICO
NICK DANGER
BUBBA
DR. DOGGE
THE NIX
SONNY
JIVE CAT
THE HAWK

PEGTER BERGMAN was   JOEY DEMOGRAPHICO
MIDGE
MR. LIVERFACE
YVES ST. STOOL
LT. BRADSHAW
IKE
POP
REVEREND DEE

DAVID OSSMAN was   GRAMPS DEMOGRAPHICO
ANNOUNCER
BEN BLAND
GENERAL STARSUCKER
LOCAL HOSTIN
FATHER
FDR
JUNIOR STARSUCKER

PHIL PROCTOR was   DAD (DON) DEMOGRAPHICO
BOSUN BOB
OFF-STAGE PRODUCER
ROCKY (RICKY) ROCOCO
BILL LUMP
ED GIBBERSON
SGT. BLOOTWURST
SECOND ANNOUNCER
HARRY

THE PLACE: The home, TV set and fantasy life of the Don Demographico family of Devo Heights, Ohio. The time is The Present.

JOEY'S HOUSE

The Overture is played, and the curtain rises.

DAD is discovered shaving in the bathroom. MOM is in bed, crying softly. GRAMPS is slumped, asleep in front of the TV set. The sound is off, but the picture is on, the light on GRAMPS face. JOEY enters, powered up after his all-night job.

JOEY: Morning everybody! I'm back from work!

DAD: That you, Joey?

JOEY: Yeah, Dad.

DAD: Well, keep it quiet, son. Your mom wants to sleep late — again!

MOM: SOBS LOUDER

JOEY: Morning, Gramps! Oh — fallen asleep in front of the set again. (HE SPOTS SNACKS ON TOP OF TV SET) Oh, boy! "Insect Chips!" My favorite, too! Mmmm! "Cucarachas — with the tangy taste of Old Mexico." I like the way the little heads pop! (EATING AND LOOKING AT THE TV GUIDE) That Power Burger and Pepsi I just ate 'll keep me up til noon! Let's see what's on . . . Oh. Good — "Lucy!" I love Lucy. She never grows old. (HE CHANGES THE CHANNELS)

DAD: (WHILE BRUSHING HIS TEETH, CUBAN ACCENT) Lucy? Lucy, where are you? (SWITCHES TO FALSETTO:) Quiet, Ricky. I'm trying to sleep late. (ALTERNATING:)
Where's little Rickey?
He's in bed too — with me!
Lucy! How many times do I got to tell you? It's not good for a 23-year-old kid to be esleepin' with his mother!
The only "e-thing" not good for him — is you!
Watch it, Lucy, or I'll come in there and play Babbaloo on your buns!
Just hold your bongos for a second there, Rickey — I got a little surprise for you.

    Oh? What's that, honey?
    I'm getting a divorce!
    A divorce! Oh, no! What're we gonna do with little Rickey?
    The lawyers say he's community property, and we'll have to divide him.
    Oh, fine. Then we can give half to Ethel and half to Fred.
    No, that's no good, Rickey.
    Why e-not?
    Because they're getting a divorce, too!
    Oh, no!

JOEY: Divorce! Oh, no!

GRAMPS: (WAKING UP) Eh? What? Say, there, Joey, boy — do your old Gramps a kindness and switch the TV. I wanna watch the PTL Club.

JOEY: Oh, yeah. "Pay The Lord."

JOEY SWITCHES THE CHANNELS AND GRAMPS DOES "WHITE NOISE" BETWEEN STATIONS, THEN:

GRAMPS: Jesus! God, I love to wake up every morning with Jesus! Jesus is so bland and wonderful. Believe in Jesus, and you've got no tricky moral problems to work out on your own. That's right — your worries are over. Just leave it all to Jeeezus! Why not give him a call — His number's right up there on your screen. And while you call, we'll pray. We'll pray for a better breakfast this morning than we got yesterday morning. We'll pray for food. A crust of bread . . .

JOEY: OK, Gramps. Let's go fix you some breakfast.

JOEY WHEELS GRAMPS OFF. DURING THE PTL SEQUENCE, DAD PUTS ON HIS WHITE DENTIST'S JACKET, TRIES TO KISS MOM GOODBYE AND IS REBUFFED. HE LEAVES IN A HUFF AS JOEY AND GRAMPS EXIT. MOM RISES FROM BED, CROSSES TO THE TV, BANGS ON IT, AND CHANGES THE CHANNELS. WATCHING THE TV, MOM BECOMES ALL THE GUESTS ON THE "DINAH!" SHOW, THEN SWITCHES CHANNELS AND DOES EXERCISES WITH "THE BODY BUILDERS." MOM, JOGGING IN PLACE, IS JOINED BY ANOTHER JOGGER, MIDGE.

MIDGE: Madge, can I talk to you for a minute?

MOM: Sure, Midge. What's the matter? Got a special problem?

MIDGE: Right on. I had a real blow-out this morning.

MOM: You mean with your test husband?

MIDGE: No, with my spare tire.

MOM: Oh, that's because you're a woman, Midge — and because I'm a woman too, I know that you have Special Product Needs.

MOM AND MIDGE PLAY GOLF.

MIDGE: Oh, does that make me Special too?

MOM: It does if you use "Special Care," Midge.

MIDGE: You mean — on those "special places?"

THE LADIES SWITCH TO TENNIS.

MOM: Especially on those "special days." Just be specially careful when you use it.

MIDGE RUNS INTO THE WALL TRYING TO RETURN A POWER-HOUSE SERVE. THE LADIES SWITCH TO TARGET PRACTICE.

MIDGE: You're right about that "Special Care," Madge. Blamm!! I blew both radials driving over the Gibberson boy this morning — Blamm!! And I didn't specially care! Blamm!! Blam!! Blamm!!

THEY BOTH SHOOT. THE ANNOUNCER IS SEEN, READING FROM HIS SCRIPT INTO A MICROPHONE.

ANN: "Special Care" — the "special" vaginal tranquilizer. For women only. (HE PAUSES FOR CUE) This is ABC — the Alien Blandcasting Clone. Look out for "The Boat People!" There's laffs galore and guns on shore, as those wonderful, warm-hearted Boat People try to land jobs at the Newport Beach Marina Club — tonight at 7! Then, it gets dirty after 12:30 on "Battle of the Hollywood Hot Tubs" — tonight! It's comedy sex at its wild and crazy best! And now — stay tuned for "The Bosun Bob Show!"

"BOSUN BOB'S" THEME MUSIC — A HORNPIPE — BEGINS, AND BOSUN BOB ENTERS WITH A BIG RED BOZO NOSE, DANCING.

BOB: Good morning, little mateys and future play-mateys! Toot, toot! Pipe me aboard! Yes, avast little sailors and sailorettes — or should I call you little "sales-persons?" Hope you're not as hungover as I am. Toot, toot! I could use a toot right now. (TAKES OFF HIS BOZO NOSE) Looks just like my own nose! Oh, well. Sometimes I wish this were a real boat instead of a set. I could throw up over the railing. But — I was celebrating my birthday last night, kids. That's right, I finally turned the big three-oh. (HE HOLDS UP THREE FINGERS)

OFFSTAGE VOICE: Hey, Bob! Give us another finger!

BOB: Alright, alright! I turned 40 — are you satisfied? That's right, 40 big ones! And twenty of 'em have been ON THIS SHOW! Pretty soon, I won't have go draw the wrinkles on anymore, right? Toot, toot! And speaking of "drawing," kids -
(HE SINGS) Let's take out our pencil box,
    Our pencil box, our pencil box!
    Open it up and take 'em out,
    And lay 'em on the floor . . .
And sit on 'em! No, I'm just kidding, kids. You don't want to sit on 'em, because you might hurt yourself — and then you'd have to buy some of those grown-up products we sell later in the day! Don't want to do that! (TALKING TO HIS PENCIL) Hey, Penny Pencil! How are you this morning? (AS PENNY) "I feel real sharp, Bosun Bob." Are you going to draw a nice picture for us today? "I sure am, Bosun Bob." Well, I hope you do, Penny, 'cause if you don't, I'll run your pretty little head through the pencil sharpener! OK, what shall we draw today? (HE LISTENS) That's a good idea, Joey! We'll draw the ship's cat, OK? It's

real easy. (DRAWING) First we draw a pear, then cover it with hair, then some footsies and a head — oh, oh! This cat is dead! (TURNS THE PICTURE UPSIDE DOWN) That's right, kids. The ship's cat dies of scurvy. So just draw his little tail curled up like this — put a little "x" for his eye, like this — and then you can put a little tag on his toe — and put the name of your own little kitty in here — and drop it in your daddy's bathtub, just like we do here at sea! OK! And we'll be right back with today's cartoon feature really soon — right after this important message for mommy. See ya in a minute, kids! Toot, toot!

HE HORNPIPES OFF. BLACKOUT. LIGHTS UP ON MR. LIVERFACE, SINGING TO HIMSELF.

MR. L: . . . and I put 'em on the grocery wall!

MOM COMES IN TO THE "BUTCHER SHOP"

MR. L: Well, well, well! What can I do for you, m'am?

MOM: Mr. Liverface? You're a butcher. You're up to your knees in fresh meat every day. What's the best food for my dog?

MR. L: Oh! What all dogs love to eat — cat!

MOM: Cat? Er, ah — ha ha ha . . .

MR. L: I'm serious. There's enough protein and minerals in a teeny kitty's body to make a big dog happy and healthy. And there's a full dead cat in every can of "Mr. Liverface's Dead Cat Dog Food!"

MOM: Well, that's all right for the little doggy, Mr. L., but what do I feed my cat?

MR. L: Dog!

MOM: (HITS HIM WITH HER PURSE) Not my dog!

MR. L:	No, no, no, m'am. But there's a full pound of ground pound hound in every can of "Mr. Liverface's Dead Dog Cat Food."
MOM:	Oh! I'll take one of each!
MR. L:	You ARE one of each!
MOM:	And one for Gramps!
MR. L:	(SINGS) Dog and cats and cats and dogs – Your pets can eat them all! I chop 'em up and stuff 'em in a can, And put 'em on the grocery wall!

AS MR. LIVERFACE LAUGHS, A BLACKOUT. THE LIGHTS COME UP ON AN EMPTY STAGE WITH A CHAIR, CENTER. "SYNCOPATED CLOCK" THEME MUSIC. BEN BLAND ENTERS.

BEN:	Good morning, everybody. Yep, it's old Ben Bland back with you again today on the all-day Movie Matinee. We've got another great second feature for you today — a real "B" movie! You know, you might be interested in knowing how they got that name — "B Movies" — well, it seems that, back a long time ago, during the silent film era, they had these giant film studios, with these very high ceilings — and up there — way up in the rafters, the bees would build nests! Now that . . .

OFF-STAGE PRODUCER: Ben . . .

BEN:	OK, right — the movie. It's an Academy Award nominee — in 1951, for Best Hat Design. Actually, I think it was for Best Hat Adapted From a Hat From Another Medium. I don't think it won anyway. Doesn't make any difference — it's a great "Nick Danger" movie — and it's called "Frame Me, Pretty" — and it stars like always, Huston Bogus, with Rex Spoffard, Patricia Zunt and Bill Ding. What an actor that Ding is! I remember . . .
PRODUCER:	Ben . . .

BEN: OK ... the Trivia Quiz! And it's a real good one today — I've got a real little surprise for you — now, here's the question — "What actor, in his younger days, appears in the role of Nick's nemesis on the boat, a little later on in the movie?" Numbers to call are right there on your screen — so, enjoy 'em! Now, let's go right on with the movie — "Frame Me, Pretty" ... (NOTHING HAPPENS) So, let's go — right now ... (NOTHING) Uh ... (LOOKS AROUND) ...

THE LIGHTS GO DOWN ON BEN, AT LAST.

NICK DANGER IS DRIVING. HIS "HEADLIGHTS" PIERCE THE DARKNESS. HIS FACE IS DIMLY LIT.

NICK: It was a day-for-night kind of night on Exterior Boulevard. I put my last dollar in the tank and bought six gallons of Ethyl — but it looked like she was running out on me. The little red needle was bouncing off "empty." I needed a fill-up bad, so I reached in my glove compartment and pulled out a glove, and sucked on two fingers of it. The sweet and sour smell of spilled bourbon mashed my brain. This old glove really had a story to tell — if only these fingers could do the talking ... The voice on the other end of the phone had promised me a job — and boy, did I need it. I'd take anything — even this baby-sitting job ... Look at these houses! I hate rich people. I hate them and their stupid problems ... (HE SHIFTS GEARS) I pulled up the slick marble driveway of Number 108 and fishtailed my car to a stop!

THE HEADLIGHTS SWERVE. A MEOW AND A DOG'S HOWL. NICK GETS OUT OF THE CAR.

NICK: Oh, oh! Hope I hit the doberman and not the cat. In the glare of the headlights stood the big house. It looked more like a movie studio, or a mortuary — only the stiffs inside could tell me which ...

NICK WALKS FROM THE CAR TO THE HOUSE. TRIPS.

NICK: Oh, my knee! Who planted this damn bonsai here?

NICK KNOCKS AT THE DOOR, WHICH CREEEKS OPEN REVEALING ROCKY ROCOCO.

ROCKY: Good evening, sir . . .

NICK: Phew! This monkey smelled like the powder room in an aircraft factory. What are you wearing?

ROCKY: French Tub Bubble Water. Light a match and it's gone.

ROCKY LIGHTS A MATCH AND THE LIGHTS COME UP.

ROCKY: Ah, it is you, Mr. Danger. (OPENS DOOR) Come inside. These hot nights — aren't they awful, Mr. Danger? The heavy smell of magnolia drives me mad. Oh, by the way, my name is Ricky . . .

NICK: Ricky Rococo?

ROCKY: Yes! It was I who called you on the phone. Now, follow me. By the way, you wouldn't have an Egyptian cigarette on you, would you?

NICK: Not on me. I keep 'em in my box at the bank.

ROCKY LEADS NICK ALONG A COMPLEX ROUTE, INCLUDING A FINAL ASCENT UP A WINDING STAIRCASE. NICK, FOLLOWING, GETS LOST. ROCKY BABBLES ON, WHILE NICK NARRATES OVER.

ROCKY: A pity! My uncle, General Starsucker, prohibits me absolutely from smoking in the Aquarium Room. Do you enjoy raising fish, Mr. Danger? I don't. I enjoy eating them, though. All except Pire-anya! They eat back! I remember . . . (HE BABBLES ON)

NICK: I had heard of Lancelot Starsucker — eccentric recluse publisher. Who hadn't? He was old money. Maybe they were going to wheel the General out for some fresh air, and they were hiring me to protect him from Dillinger!

ROCKY IS A DISTANCE AWAY FROM NICK. HE TURNS BACK AND LOOKS FOR HIM.

ROCKY: Mr. Danger? Where are you? I'm over here!

NICK: So am I.

BOTH: Keep talking and I'll follow the sound of your voice. (PAUSE) OK! Wait a minute — let's not talk at the same time. What? This is never going to work . . .

ROCK AND NICK HAVE RETRACED THEIR STEPS. THEY SUDDENLY BUMP INTO ONE ANOTHER.

BOTH: Ah! There you are!

NICK: Who built this place? An architect, or the Army Corps of Engineers? Where are the tank traps?

ROCKY: Ha ha. Very jolly. Excuse me — I hope this is not going to upset you, Mr. Danger, but before we proceed any further, I'm afraid I'm going to have to frisk you. (HE PULLS OUT HIS GUN)

NICK: Oh. It has a widdle gun.

ROCKY: Shut up! Ricky says, "Put your hands up." (NICK DOES SO) Now, open your coat. (NICK DOESN'T) I'll kill you! Open your coat!

NICK: Say, "Ricky says."

ROCKY: What? Open your coat!

NICK: Say, "Ricky says, open your coat."

ROCKY: Ricky says open your coat. (NICK DOES) That's better! Ah ha!

ROCKY PULLS OUT NICK'S PISTOL. HE HOLDS IT OUT TO NICK.

ROCKY: Hold this.

NICK: Ricky says . . .

ROCKY: Yes, Ricky says "hold this!" And Ricky says "hold this too."

SEARCHING HIM. RICKY PULLS OUT THE GLOVE, AND THEN A CIGARETTE.

ROCKY: And Ricky says, "Ah ha!" You were holding out on me all this time, weren't you, Nick?

ROCKY LIGHTS HIS CIGARETTE WITH HIS OWN GUN — A TRICK LIGHTER. HE EXPLODES WITH COUGHING.

NICK: Just because there's a camel on it doesn't mean it's Egyptian.

ROCKY: Get inside!

ROCKY PUSHES NICK AHEAD OF HIM AND THEY ENTER THE "AQUARIUM ROOM" WHERE GENERAL STARSUCKER APPEARS TO SNOOZE IN HIS WHEELCHAIR, A SLEEP MASK OVER HIS FACE. ROCKY HAS HIS LIGHTER-GUN ON NICK. STARSUCKER LIFTS HIS MASK TO REVEAL HIS EYEPATCH.

STAR: You may put your hands down now, Mr. Danger.

NICK: Thanks, General.

NICK, HIS GUN STILL IN HIS UPRAISED HAND, LOWERS IT AND CONKS ROCKY ON THE HEAD.

ROCKY: Ow! Ricky says I'll get you for that, Danger!

STAR: Scuttle back to your hole, nephew!

ROCKY: Ricky says, he's leaving . . . (HE EXITS ALONG AN ELABORATE ROUTE) He's going . . . he's going . . . he's gone.

STAR: As you see, Mr. Danger, I'm trapped in this chair like a toad in a hole, so your bodyguarding job promises not to be too difficult.

NICK: Yeah, but who keeps their promises these days?

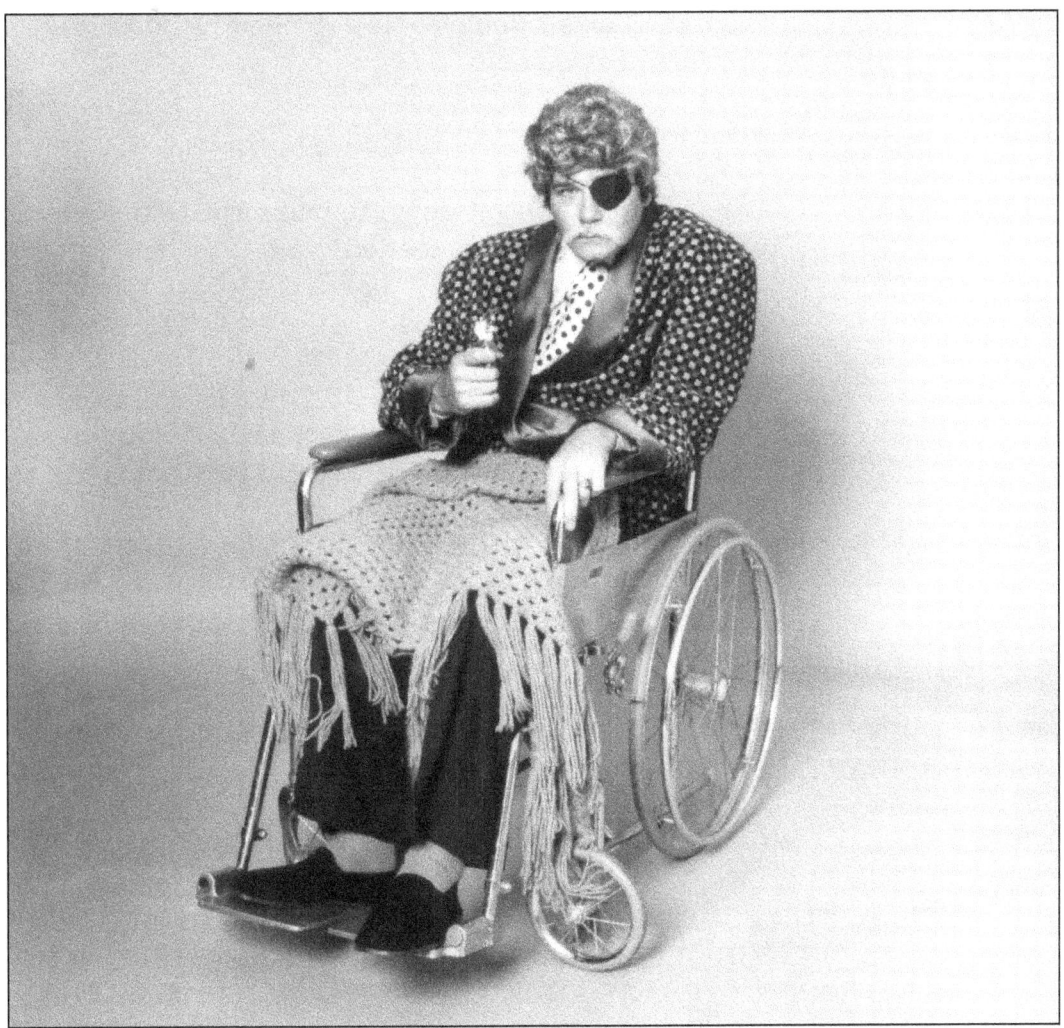

STAR: Hum! Everybody likes a detective with a sense of humor, Mr. Danger.

NICK: I don't. Not enough money in it. And speaking of money, I get 35 dollars a day, and some of it in advance.

STAR: Ah, money! I love the feel of money — like the skin of dead men, with dead men's pictures printed on it. It's all I have left.

HE TOSSES NICK A THICK ROLL OF BILLS.

NICK: There's a lot of 35 dollars a day in here — and from what I've seen so far, I don't think I'm going to last on the job.

STAR: Take it, Danger. You're going to need it. Good lawyers cost money.

NICK: What? Are you nuts?

STAR: Far from it. Let's get down to business. Is that fine oiled weapon of yours loaded?

NICK: Sure — I'm always loaded.

STAR: May I? (NICK HANDS THE GUN OVER) Ah, I see it's a Japanese Kreuger. They don't make these anymore. I hear they're not accurate beyond two feet.

NICK STEPS BACK A FOOT AS THE GENERAL HOLDS THE GUN ON HIM.

STAR: But that hardly seems to matter anymore, now does it?

THE GENERAL SUDDENLY TURNS THE GUN ON HIMSELF AND FIRES INTO HIS HEART, POINT-BLANK.

NICK: General!

NICK GOES TO THE BODY, SLUMPED IN THE WHEELCHAIR, BENDS OVER IT AND PICKS HIS PISTOL OUT OF THE GENERAL'S HAND. AS HE DOES SO, ROCKY APPEARS AND TAKES A FLASH PHOTO OF THE SCENE.

ROCKY: Ricky says, "He's got you now, Danger!"

AS ROCKY LAUGHS HYSTERICALLY, NICK STANDS CAUGHT WITH GUN AND MONEY IN HAND. NICK AND STARSUCKER ARE CAUGHT IN THE SPOTLIGHT — AN INTENSE DRAMATIC IMAGE. THE LIGHTS SUDDENLY GO UP TO COLOR TV STRENGTH AND THE BACKGROUND MUSIC CHANGES FROM MOODY TO "FASHION SHOW." NICK AND STARSUCKER TAKE A BOW AND LEAVE THE STAGE. THEY ARE FASHION MODELS. AS THEY GO OUT, LOCAL HOSTIN AND YVES ST. STOOL ENTER. LOCAL ASKS FOR AUDIENCE APPLAUSE.

LOCAL: Aren't they wonderful? Isn't he wonderful? "Mondo Macho" by Yves St. Stool! "Le Mood Detectif." The latest in Celebrity Fashions. Well, let's just sit down, Yves, so we can talk.

YVES:	The models, Local, were Fifi and Hernandez — they flew all the way here from St. Insincere . . .
LOCAL:	That's just beautiful! And you tell me that these are going to be the styles for the Eighties — the styles that are going to "say the unsayable."
YVES:	Yes, celebrities are everywhere now. And it is the function of the celebrity to dress like celebrities and to be seen speaking as loudly and incessantly as possible — in my clothes! And that includes you.
LOCAL:	Well, I don't think of myself as really being a celebrity . . .
YVES:	Oh, come now, Local . . .
LOCAL:	I eat with celebrities, I talk with celebrities, I sleep with celebrities, but . . .
YVES:	"Local Hostin! Local Hostin!" That is your name! Your name is flashing on the show! I see your name

everywhere! That is the secret of celebrity, n'est-ce pas?

LOCAL: But your name — it's a household word! "Stool!" Yves St. Stool!

YVES: That is because I put my name on everything I make — chairs, diapers, glasses, lovers — it doesn't matter. But let me tell you something. There is a lot of pain in being a celebrity, because when you are so high, you have an overview and you can see what is coming! And I can see what is coming in this country and it's not very good!

LOCAL: Now, we were talking about this backstage before the show, and Yves is a very serious person. He's a very concerned celebrity and we were talking — of course, all of you have been talking — about the Energy Crisis. And I know that Yves can say — will say — the Unsayable. And he's going to say it right now, for you, on this show.

YVES: Thank you, Local. You know, I feel comfortable to say it around you. You know that there is just not enough energy to go around anymore. So, if you are too old, if you are too sick, if you are too unemployable, if you are just too wasted — sooner or later, we are going to have to turn the lights out on you!

LOCAL: There! That's saying the Unsayable!

HE LEADS THE AUDIENCE IN APPLAUSE.

YVES: Thank you. Merci.

LOCAL: And now, for our next guest on the show — a former football great, now a Las Vegas actor — the great "Bubba!"

HE LEADS THE APPLAUSE AS BUBBA SAUNTERS IN

LOCAL: Lovely to have you, Bubba — on my show, I mean — and, Bubba — I just have to say how great you were

	last week when you starred in that episode of "The Love Boat People!"
YVES:	He was "un enfant terrible," Local, he really was!
LOCAL:	All right, I know you were listening backstage, so I want to know what you think, right now, about Yves' ideas on the Energy Crisis.
BUBBA:	Well, Merv, I think that I probably don't agree, but again I might agree — but I probably don't — with what he has to say. But on the other hand, I think that it probably is, or perhaps is not, inevitable. I think, then, that it's the fan that's important in this — in our industry — in this industry of ours. And I think that the fan would like to be pleased and wants things done right — even if it's being done to him!
LOCAL:	No celebrity could disagree with that! (LEADS THE APPLAUSE) You know, speaking of energy — I don't often remember jokes, but I did hear one recently, and that reminds me of it. I wonder if you know how many Californians it takes to screw in a light bulb?
YVES:	I know! It takes none. Because a light bulb is too small a place to SCREW in!
LOCAL:	No . . . er, that's not it. Er, Bubba?
BUBBA:	Lemme he'p ya out here, Hoss! We rehearsed this in the green room. "Yes, Johnny, how many Californians DOES it take to screw in a light bulb?"
LOCAL:	Eight.
BUBBA:	Eight?
LOCAL:	Yes. It takes one to screw it in, three to relate to the experience and four more to turn it into a television pilot! Isn't that wonderful?
YVES:	I don't get it. Why don't we talk about something I'm interested in, like shoes? I'm introducing my all-new,

solar-powered imitation microwave boots. You see here? (HE DEMONSTRATES) It has the little live octopus in the see-through heel. When you go walking down Rodeo Drive or Park Avenue, you put the squeeze on the squid, and the PAIN generates electricity, and this electricity runs the boot and lights up my initials on the side! They're $5000 a pair at Neiman Markup! Right across from the bank.

LOCAL: Well, what do you think of these boots, Bubba?

BUBBA: Well, sir — I appreciate fashion. I wear boots, of course.

YVES: Boots! Is that what you call that pair of sandboxes you've got on? You are a celebrity, and it's the duty of a celebrity to publically spend as much money on goods and clothes as possible! Otherwise this country is going to slip into this kind of petit-bourgeois, gray, nauseating style that I see everywhere! I mean, just having to look at the way you dress, Bubba — it makes me want to throw up! (HE IS REALLY GOING TO) And . . . there's a little place . . . urp! . . . here in my boots to do it . . . (AND HE DOES)

THERE IS A BEAT OF AMAZED SILENCE. YVES WIPES HIS MOUTH ON HIS SLEEVE. LOCAL RECOVERS:

LOCAL: Bubba? You have an expression of amazement on your face! Do you — do you like these boots?

BUBBA: You know, I — it occurs to me that this semi-intelligent double-brained frog here has just insulted me! Of course, we're all celebrities here — and I guess I enjoy boots as much as the next man. I fact, I would love to take those Microwave Octopus Boots of yours . . .

YVES: You like these?

BUBBA: And shove them right up your microwave (BLANK), you stupid mother-(BLANK)!

YVES: I did not come here to be insulted by some merde-kicking rouge-neck!

BUBBA AND YVES ARGUE, WORDS HEAVILY CENSORED WITH (BLANKS). LOCAL LOOKS ON, HAVING A WONDERFUL TIME. THE "CAMERA" PULLS IN ON LOCAL:

LOCAL: Well, that certainly is exciting! Isn't Las Vegas just wonderful? But don't go away now, because I'll be right back with a credit dentist who's going to law school, right after this nice word. Don't go way . . .

A BLACKOUT. LIGHTS COME UP ON NEWSMAN BILL LUMP.

LUMP: It's the Noon News Break with me, Bill Lump. And these are today's top stories: Latest pictures from Hell confound NASA scientists as the Satan One Hell Probe reveals an atmosphere composed of hairspray, cigarette smoke and solid air freshener. From Mexico, more horror stories are forthcoming on the plight of illegal American oil-pickers. The octopus alert along the Southern California coast continues unabated. And, a local credit dentist, "Doctor Dee," is charged for allegedly performing oral prophylaxis on unconscious patients! We'll have those stories and more, later on the 4:30, 5:35, 6:05, 6:55, 7:00, 7:30, 7:45 and 5-before-8 o'clock News — with the All-New News Attack Team: Me, Bill Lump — Connie Hunk — and the heartbreakingly beautiful Volvo Toyoto! "News before you eat, news while you eat, news after you eat — more news than you can ever digest!" But first, stay tuned now for another dramatic episode of my favorite soap, "Lawyer's Hospital."

A BLACKOUT. LIGHTS COME UP ON MIDGE, TALKING TO HERSELF, AS SHE UNDERGOES A DESPARATE EMOTIONAL CRISIS:

MIDGE: Don't go mad — don't be sad, Midge. Midge? Midge! That's me! Don't be sad, don't go mad — don't go over the edge, Midge. They need you, Midge. I need you! Do I? Am I? Oh, Midge, Midge, Midge, Midge — hold on! This hell can't go on forever! Even if it does!

DR. DON ENTERS. IT'S DAD. HE'S JUST COME OUT OF SURGERY.

DR. DON: Midge? Midge? Is that you?

MIDGE: I think so, Dr. Don.

DR. DON: Well, your father looks like he's going to make it.

MIDGE: Yes, I'm so glad. If he'd have died, it would have killed him.

DR. DON: And don't worry that pretty little head of yours about the Gibberson boy. I just removed one of those radials from his larynx.

MIDGE: He's a very special boy . . .

DR. DON: He is now . . .

MIDGE NOTICES THAT DR. DON HAS SOMETHING HORRIBLE ON HIS SHOULDER. IT'S HIS GLOVE. SHE SCREAMS!

DR. DON: Midge, Midge! Don't come apart on me now! You've been very brave and very, very beautiful through all of this, and we don't often see that here at Lawyer's Hospital. Oh, yes — the doctors are brave and the lawyers are beautiful, but to see them both together in one — package! It's enough to make a married doctor like me become addicted.

DR. DON STROKES MIDGE'S LEG WITH WHAT APPEARS TO BE A SEVERED HAND.

DR. DON: But I have medicine and science, science and medicine. Not that I'm not a man like anyone else, who likes nice boots and beautiful women. But let's just keep that our "little secret," OK?

MIDGE: (TRYING TO SPEAK — THE HAND IS OVER HER MOUTH) Mrrrrrfffffle . . .

DR. DON: Good. Well, I gotta go.

MIDGE: Don't leave me now, Don!

DR. DON: I've got to go — to a very special patient.

MIDGE: You mean — to Bambi?

DR. DON: I'm not mean to Bambi. She likes it that way!

DR. DON SLAPS MIDGE ACROSS THE FACE WITH HIS RUBBER GLOVES AND STALKS OUT. MIDGE GOES INTO HYSTERICS. DR. DOGGE ENTERS, WHEELING FATHER, WHOSE HEAD IS TURBANNED WITH BANDAGES. DR. DOGGE GIVES FATHER A GOOD-BYE PAT ON TOP OF THE HEAD AND LEAVES. FATHER REACTS VIOLENTLY TO THE PAT AND MIDGE NOTICES HIM.

MIDGE: Oh, Father! Was the electro-shock therapy everything you expected?

FATHER: I — I — I — I don't remember . . .

MIDGE: Father, you're so brave — and look at me! I'm coming apart like a little shattered teapot!

AS FATHER TALKS, MIDGE WHEELS HIM ACROSS AND TO THE VERY EDGE OF THE STAGE, FALLING ASLEEP ON THE WAY.

FATHER: Oh, come, Midge. Tell me your problem, and take your time, dear — because if there's anything I ever was, or ever will be, or ever COULD be to you, Midge, it's a strong, steady, loving, faithful, listening, relating, sensitive, doting influence on . . . (ON THE EDGE) Midge!!

MIDGE: (RECOVERING) I'm sorry, Father.

FATHER: We nearly went — over the edge! Together! Are you feeling better now?

MIDGE: Yes, rested.

FATHER: Then what's your problem? Is it — that Gibberson boy?

MIDGE: He's not the Gibberson boy anymore, Father. He was sold over the TV to that priest by a mercenary.

FATHER: He was?

MIDGE: Was he?

FATHER: That's right, he was — wasn't he? Did — did you tell me that, Midge?

MIDGE: Yes, I did. I told you last week — yesterday.

FATHER: That's right. That's when you had that flashback, wasn't it? We — we're still in that flashback, now, aren't we?

MIDGE: (SOBBING) I — I don't know. I don't know anything anymore!

MIDGE AND FATHER GO OUT, SHE PUSHING HIM AND SOBBING. AS THEY LEAVE, DR. DON AND DR. DOGGE ENTER.

DR. DON: You know, Dr. Dogge, I feel terrible.

DOGGE: Don't worry, that Gibberson boy will pull through.

DR. DON: No, it's not about him. I feel terrible. Jumbo fixed up some Chicken-in-a-Body-Bag last night. Urp! And I don't think it was quite dead. I'd like you to pump me out before we go to lunch.

DOGGE: Yes. Of course. Right this way . . .

THE MUSIC SURGES AND THE DOCTORS EXIT AS THE LIGHTS GO TO A BLACKOUT.

DISCO THEME UNDER

GAL: What's happening in StarSucker this week? His press aide tells why the President is afraid of his own suit!

YVES: What do Farrah and Groucho have in common — besides that mustache?

GAL: What do psychics say about raising snakes as temporary office workers?

YVES: And just for us StarSuckers — the new Dr. Lustface Liver Diet. Plus, Ayatolla Khomeini tells us how to cut off sexism . . .

GAL:	Before it starts! Mais oui! It's StarSucker — bigger than LIFE and hipper than Hustler!
YVES:	In the sugar and cigarette section where you shop.
GAL & YVES:	I read mine — in line!

MUSIC UP AND OUT

WHEN THE LIGHTS GO UP, BEN BLAND IS SEEN, TALKING ON THE PHONE:

BEN:	Yes, m'am. Right. No, it wasn't Orson Welles. Well, he's my favorite too, but he just isn't in this picture. No. Thank you. (HANGS UP) That puts our Trivia Jackpot up another five dollars — there's about enough in there now to get a tank of gas, if you had someplace to go. We'll take another call later, but first, here's a word from the "Handgun School of Truckstopping."
PRODUCER:	Ben . . .
BEN:	Oh, OK. How about another nice word from the folks at new "Spoil 'n' Broil's New Chicken In A Body Bag."
PRODUCER:	Read your card, Ben . . .
BEN:	Ah, that's right — we'd like you all to tune in tonight at . . .
PRODUCER:	8:00 o'clock . . .
BEN:	Eight o'clock, right — wherever that might be in your Time Zone, for the Danny Lewis-Jerry Thomas Telethon for Musical Discophy. Hmmm . . . well, we've all got to dance sometime . . .
PRODUCER:	Read it again, Ben . . .
BEN:	Ah, it's the Nuclear Disastrophy Disco Telethon. OK, Nuclear Disastrophy, tonight at 8:00 o'clock, wherever you are. I'll be back, after this . . .

BEN LOOKS BEFUDDLED AS THE LIGHTS FADE TO A BLACKOUT.
THEY COME UP ON ED GIBBERSON.

ED: (SINGS) It's Ed Gibberson's Crazy Owl Market
But the Civil Defense Department is mine! Yes, we've scraped to the bare bottom of our overstocked shelter to bring up the lowest of super-low low values to you! Special all this week at Gibberson's — 50-gallon drums of water in heavy syrup, just 50 cents a dozen! Truckloads of crates of busted boxes of broken crackers, 5 dollars a truck-load, and you can keep the truck! And — giant Galvanized Hams, hopelessly rusted together in lots of about 20, for about 20 cents a lot, and that's not a lot! Not at Gibberson's, where the prices will drive you mad! So reach through the TV and grab the first person you see . . .

ED REACHES OUT AND PULLS IN JOEY, WHO IS AMAZED AND PLEASED.

ED: And bring 'em on down to Gibberson's where (HE SINGS) The Owl Department, the Octopus Department, the Insect Department — the whole fuckin' store is mine!

JOEY SINGS ALONG WITH THE SONG, WHICH ENDS WITH A BLACKOUT. WHEN THE LIGHTS COME UP, JOEY IS STILL STANDING THERE, LOOKING SURPRISED. BEN BLAND IS BACK IN HIS CHAIR. HE LOOKS WITH CONFUSION UPON JOEY AND ASKS, SOTTO VOCE:

BEN: Who is he? Is this my guest?

PRODUCER: Don't know, Ben . . .

BEN: Who are you, young man?

JOEY; I'm Joey Demographico — your average viewer.

BEN: How old are you?

JOEY: Male, 18 to 25.

BEN: Where do you come from, Joey?

JOEY: Devo Hights, Ohio.

BEN: Well . . . what sort of thing do you do there?

JOEY: Nothing. I work all night at the Burger King and then I watch TV most of the day. I was watching TV just now and a guy put his hand through the screen and pulled me right in!

BEN: I know that ad — Gibberson's — drives me nuts!

JOEY: I kinda like it. It got me on TV. Say, what channel are we on?

BEN: I don't know. This part of the show is syndicated.

PRODUCER: Ben . . .

BEN: Look, son, why don't you just pick up your chair and go over there and you can watch the rest of the movie, OK?

JOEY: Can you get me in the movies?

BEN: You're lucky you're on television.

JOEY: So are you.

JOEY WANDERS OFF TOWARD BACKSTAGE.

BEN: Now, back to our great "B" movie . . .

JOEY: Hey! There's a bottle of liquor back here.

BEN: Sure. It's a prop for a commercial. OK. Here's Nick Danger in part two of "Frame Me, Pretty."

BEN LEANS BACK TO SEE WHAT'S HAPPENING WITH JOEY AS THE LIGHTS FADE TO A BLACKOUT. WHEN THEY COME UP, NICK DANGER IS REVEALED, SEATED, HANDCUFFED TO POLICE SGT. BLOOTWURST, WHO STANDS GUARD WHILE DOING A CROSSWORD PUZZLE. NICK "NARRATES:"

NICK: When you're framed this pretty, they usually hang you in a museum. But why me? I kept asking myself the same question over and over again. Why? Why did he do it? And I wasn't the only one asking questions, either . . .

BLOOT: Hey, Danger?

NICK: Yeah?

BLOOT: What's a three-letter word for "ant?"

POLICE LT. BRADSHAW ENTERS.

BRAD: All right, Blootwurst. Take the cuffs off him.

BLOOT: Right, Lt. Bradshaw.

BRAD: I can handle any two-bit gumshoe. All right, Danger, you . . .

BLOOT: Excuse me, chief?

BRAD: What is it?

BLOOT: Can I take the cuffs off of me, too?

BRAD: Yeah. Take them off. Now, Danger — this is the happiest day of my life . . .

BLOOT: Chief?

BRAD: What is it?

BLOOT: You didn't give me the key to the other cuff.

BRAD: It's in the car. Next to the siren.

BLOOT: That's right, chief.

BRAD: Blootwurst!

BLOOT: I'm going, sir . . .

BLOOTWURST LEAVES.

BRAD: He's gone. Now, Danger . . .

FROM OFF, A POLICE SIREN WAILS.

BLOOT: (FROM OFF) Sorry, chief!

BRAD: Now, where was I?

NICK: It's the happiest day in your life.

BRAD: That's right, Danger — cause I'm gonna send ya to the hotseat!

NICK: I didn't do it, Bradshaw!

BRAD: You didn't do it? You're standing in the dead man's aquarium with a hundred-thousand clams in yer mitts and a smokin' gat with your prints all over it! And we got a picture of it, taken by the victim's nephew, a respectable magnolia importer. And you're tryin' to tell me you didn't do it? Then whose picture is this?

NICK: (LOOKING AT THE PHOTO) This is a picture of Joan Crawford, tied up in a child's bed.

BRAD: (CHECKING IT) Oh, yeah? That's a good one! Say, have you seen the one of Heddy Lamarr and FDR on some hot springs? (ANOTHER PHOTO) But this is the one that's goin' on the front page!

NICK: Hey, it's me, Bradshaw — Nick Danger! You gotta give me a chance to clear myself. Give me 24 hours, at least.

BRAD: In 24 hours, Danger, the man who captured General Starsucker's cold-blooded killer is gonna be runnin' for District Attorney. (HE'S GOT THE ROLL OF MONEY IN HIS HAND) And here's my campaign kitty! I'm gonna be D. A. and you're gonna be D. O. A.! (HE PULLS OUT HIS GUN) You died escapin' — ain't it a shame?

NICK: Wait a minute. Isn't there another way to handle this? Can't I make a little campaign contribution?

BRAD: How much?

NICK: A buck . . .

WITH THAT, NICK BUTTS BRADSHAW IN THE BALLS. BRADSHAW DOUBLES UP AND NICK MAKES TO ESCAPE.

BRAD: Hey, Nick! Hold it, hold it! I was gonna let you go. Can't ya take a joke?

NICK: A joke?

BRAD: Sure. And here's the punchline!

CATCHING NICK OFF-GUARD, BRADSHAW LANDS A SOLID LEFT. NICK COLLAPSES IN THE CHAIR.

BRAD: Blootwurst!

BLOOTWURST COMES IN, NOW HOPELESSLY HANDCUFFED, BUT WITH A TRUNCHEON IN ONE HAND.

BLOOT: What is it, chief?

BRAD: Finish him off!

BLOOT: You bet, chief!

BLOOTWURST SWINGS HIS TRUNCHEON BACK AND IT COLD-COCKS BRADSHAW, WHO DROPS TO THE FLOOR. NICK TAKES HIS OPPORTUNITY TO ESCAPE. BLOOTWURST KNEELS TO HELP BRADSHAW.

BLOOT: Aw, chief!

BRAD: Forget me! Get him!

BLOOT: Right, chief!

BLOOTWURST DROPS BRADSHAW AND TAKES OFF AS THE LIGHTS GO TO A BLACKOUT. OUT OF THE DARKNESS, NICK COMES DRIVING, TWO "HEADLIGHTS" BLAZING. BEHIND HIM COMES BLOOTWURST, "HEADLIGHTS," REVOLVING RED LIGHT AND SIREN.

NICK: Damn! That idiot Blootwurst had handcuffed himself to the patrol car's steering wheel and he was tailing me!

BLOOT: Pull over, Danger!

NICK: Not on your life, Blootwurst!

NICK SHOOTS OVER HIS SHOULDER AT BLOOTWURST. HE BLOWS OUT ONE OF THE "HEADLIGHTS" AND BOTH CARS SWERVE.

BLOOT: You're a dead man now, Danger!

BLOOTWURST FIRES SEVERAL SHOTS AT DANGER. NICK'S TIRE IS SHOT OUT. HIS CAR SKIDS DANGEROUSLY AND CRASHES, TILTING ON

ITS SIDE. BLOOTWURST PULLS UP WITH A SCREECH, JUMPS OUT AND HOLDS A FLASHLIGHT ON DANGER'S FACE. THE DETECTIVE IS LYING PRONE.

BLOOT: All right, Danger! Hold it right there!

THE TABLEAU HOLDS FOR A MOMENT. THE ANNOUNCER APPEARS AT HIS MICROPHONE.

ANNOUNCER: Yes, hold it right there! Is this the kind of man you'd like to be caught out with late at night? If the answer is "no," let Detective Dating Service take over the search for that missing person in YOUR life . . .

BLOOTWURST'S FLASHLIGHT SEARCHES THE AUDIENCE, THEN RESTS ON A RANDOM MALE.

ANN: Now, here's an attractive young man. He says he's 30 years old, makes over 40 thousand a year in unreported income, always seems to have pretty good cocaine, and is looking for girls who love other girls! And Detective Dating has found her!

THE FLASHLIGHT PICKS OUT A FEMALE IN THE HOUSE.

ANN: She SAYS she's 22, wears edible underwear and loves TV's. She claims she started dating at 16, but we've got film on her at 11!

THE LIGHT SEARCHES THE AUDIENCE.

ANN: So whether you're investigating for Girls or Guys, Dogs or Bi's — you'll always get your match with Detective Dating Service!

THE LIGHT GOES OUT.

ANN: This is the Ceaseless B.S. Television Network. Laff it up with Ike and Dick as Harry lets loose with a big one on "Thank You, Mr. President," tonight at 8:30. But first, it's time for "Joey's House," with Devo Heights' favorite young adult — Joey Demographico. . .

A BLACKOUT. WHEN THE LIGHTS COME UP, JOEY IS SEATED IN FRONT OF THE TV, WATCHING THE END OF A BASEBALL GAME. ENTHUSIASTIC, HE FANTASIZES HE IS THE PITCHER. HE CALLS HIS OWN PLAY AND WINDS UP ON THE "MOUND." HE PITCHES. THERE IS A HORRIBLE CRY FROM OFF-STAGE. GRAMPS ENTERS WITH A BASEBALL IN HIS MOUTH.

JOEY: Say! Great catch, Gramps! All that dogfood you've been eating has made you a real retriever!

GRAMPS, GAGGED WITH THE BALL, THREATENS JOEY WITH HIS CANE.

JOEY: Oh! You want to play ball! I'll pitch, you bat!

GRAMPS: (SPITTING THE BALL OUT) No, Joey! Goldang it! I just come down to watch the News and take a little snooze before dinner. (HE SWITCHES THE CHANNELS) Oooooop! Look at them squids! Why, them poor people won't be able to drive home from work tonight! Well, Connie and Brent will tell 'em what to do. There's the numbers to call . . . (HE FALLS ASLEEP)

JOEY: Come on, Gramps! Dad! Dad, Gramps is pretending to be dead in front of the TV again and the new network shows are on and he knows I get credit at school for watching!

DAD: (ENTERING) Come on, Joey, sit down over here and leave poor Grandad alone. The TV is one of the last pleasures he has in life. And besides, if you wake him up, you could kill him!

JOEY: Well, I don't care! That's right! I just don't care anymore! This whole house is turning into a bunch of sleepwalkers!

DAD: Quiet, Joey. I'm trying to read the TV guide.

MOM ENTERS. SHE IS STILL IN HER NIGHTGOWN AND LOOKS EVEN MORE DISTRACTED AND LIKE A TENNESSEE WILLIAMS HEROINE THAN EVER.

MOM: Flores . . . flores para los muertos . . .

DAD: Now look what you've done! You woke up Mother!

JOEY: She's been watching Mexican television again, hasn't she, Dad?

DAD: (COMFORTING MOM) Yes, Joey . . .

JOEY: But you told me the doctor said she was cured!

DAD: Joey, she was cured. But then she started watching those Mexican soap operas in the maid's room. It's just a minor flashback, son . . .

JOEY: Dad, listen! I gotta get out of this house! I gotta get into a major Arbitron Sweep Area, Dad!

DAD: What the hell are you talking about?

JOEY: Dad, if I don't get famous soon, I'll go nuts!

DAD: Joey, how the heck can you get famous in Cleveland?

JOEY:	Leave!
DAD:	Leave?
JOEY:	Leave!
MOM:	(*DISTRAIT*, SINGING) Those Autumn leaves drift by my teevee, those Autumn leaves of blue and gold . . .
DAD:	Now look what you've done! She thinks she's on a variety program!
MOM:	Thank you, Dinah . . .
JOEY:	Mom, I didn't say "leaf," I said "leave!" I'm gonna leave this house!
MOM:	Joey's going to leave?
DAD:	Joey!
MOM:	You can't afford to leave, honey. You signed an open-ended contract. You're the star of this turkey!
JOEY:	What are you saying, Mom?
MOM:	I don't even have that power! I'll renegotiate my contract! Get my agent on the phone! You call your people! Joey, Joey, Joey!
JOEY:	What is it, Ma?
MOM:	Look at me, Joey, baby . . .

HE DOES. SHE CRAFTILY OPENS HER NEGLIGEE TO HIM, "EXPOSING" HERSELF. SHE EXITS BABBLING. DAD FOLLOWS HER, LEAVING THE AGHAST JOEY AND SLEEPING GRAMPS.

JOEY:	See what she did? She jiggled at me! She's trying to drive me crazy so I won't leave! Gramps? Gramps! You can help me. You're sitting on a bundle . . .
GRAMPS:	(WAKING) Umph! Not anymore. I had my bundles removed and put in Shadow Valley Savings.

JOEY: You gotta help me. I gotta dream!

GRAMPS: You don't have a cigar, do ya? A real cigar?

JOEY: Gramps, listen — I gotta dream! And I've got to start dreaming it soon or I'm gonna wake up asleep on my feet like everyone else in Devo Heights! I gotta get out. I gotta get to Hollywood and form my own independent TV production company to foster, encourage and promote a multi-cultural view of society that combats racism, sexism, negative stereotyping-ism and economic depravity-ism! And I'll call the shots! Well? What do you think of that?

GRAMPS: (WAKING) What?

JOEY: (DESPAIRING) Nobody is listening to me!

ANNOUNCER: We'll be right back to "Joey's House" right after this . . .

JOEY IS LEFT ON STAGE. A BLACKOUT. WHEN THE LIGHTS COME UP HE IS ALONE, BUT GREATLY CHANGED.

JOEY: Hey, listen to me! I'm Joey Demographico from "Joey's House." But that's not my real house, you know — this is. How do I know? 'Cause I own it! How do I know I own it? 'Cause I just sold it! Hey, I didn't want to sell — I grew up in this house. My grandfather was born in that ice-chest. My father built that gun-closet himself and lived there during the entire Second World War. And my Mother still lives upstairs in — in that room . . .

MOM: (OFF) Arrrrrrrrrrgggggghhhhhhh!

JOEY: Naw, I didn't want to sell. But then I met the expert from Balloon 2000 Realty. He showed me so much money I knew I had to move. And you will, too, when you meet the man from Balloon 2000!

AN OFF-STAGE BELL DING-DONGS.

JOEY: There he is now, with the new owners — the Ding

Dongs. They're the first Boat People on the block. So long, folks. I'm getting up and out of here, thanks to Balloon 2000!

A BLACKOUT. THE LIGHTS COME UP ON BEN BLAND.

BEN: OK . . . back again with the All-Day, All-Night Movie Matinee and — there's no winner in the Trivia Quiz?

OFF-STAGE PRODUCER: No winner, Ben . . .

BEN: OK. No winner in the Quiz. And that means we're gonna put another Gibberson quarter-half-roasted fresh owl in the Jackpot for tomorrow. By the way, the correct answer is — me! That's right! Ol' Ben Bland has a little part there as the bad guy. This was when I was under contract about 30 years ago and I made about three pictures then and . . .

PRODUCER: Ben . . .

BEN: OK. Time for another word from Napkin Extender. Oops . . . no? How about Stud Springs, the homey men's only retirement ranch paradise . . . No? OK, Well, here's the thrilling conclusion of "Frame Me, Pretty" with Huston Bogus, Bill Ding and — me . . .

WHEN THE LIGHTS COME UP, WE ARE ON BOARD THE STARSUCKER YACHT AT NIGHT. ROCKY IS AT THE WHEEL. HE ROCKS BACK AND FORTH WITH THE SEA. JUNIOR STARSUCKER COMES ON DECK.

JR: Ricky? Have you seen the signal yet, off Point Doom?

ROCKY: No, Mr. Junior. I've seen nothing yet. But you can't count on me — the heady reek of the magnolias and the opium poppies from our illegal cargo is seriously affecting my sense of direction . . .

JR: I'll take a look. Hold her steady.

ROCKY: How do I do that?

JR: Stop moving your hands.

ROCKY:	Oh. This navigating is easy once you get a handle on it!
JR:	(LOOKING OUT TO SEA) There's the signal. Oh, oh, it's red . . . Wait a minute — it's gone yellow. There, now it's green. They're sending their man Gomez to test the stuff. Stop the motor and weigh the anchor.
ROCKY:	I can't, Boss. My scales are down below, with the opium.
JR.	Never mind! Give me the wheel.
ROCKY:	(HE HANDS IT OVER) Here, boss.
JR.	No, no, no! Get below and slice up a few opium pods.
ROCKY:	I love the smell of opium. It's magnolias that drive me mad!

ROCKY LEAVES. IN THE DISTANCE A MOTORBOAT IS HEARD APPROACHING. THE "BOAT" IS PILOTED BY NICK DANGER, WHO COMES THROUGH THE AUDIENCE TOWARD THE STAGE.

JR.	All right, Gomez, cut your engine. Cut your engine! I said, cut your . . .

NICK PLOWS ON, FINALLY CRASHING INTO THE STAGE, WHICH ROCKS THE "YACHT." JUNIOR ROCKS WITH THE IMPACT.

JR:	Blasted idiot!

JUNIOR EXTENDS HIS HAND OVER THE SIDE TO NICK.

JR:	Welcome aboard "The Perfect Alibi," Mr. Gomez. We've never met, but my name is Junior Starsucker. Encantado.
NICK:	Costawages, amigo. I spell my name D-E-N-G-A-R.

NICK PULLS HIS PISTOL AS SOON AS HE IS ON BOARD. JUNIOR BACKS UP. THE YACHT ROCKS.

JR:	"Dengar." Are you an Egyptian?

NICK:	No, I'm an American. Neck Danger! And you're going to get this worm off the hook your father put me on.
JR:	How did you get away from the police?
NICK:	I took Glendale Boulevard to Alvarado, Alvarado to Western, Western to Exposition, and Exposition led me right to you! Listen, I know your father made a deal with Bradshaw to frame me, but why did he nail himself to do it? What's the real picture?

UNBEKNOWNST TO NICK, ROCKY IS COMING ON, COVERING DANGER WITH HIS PISTOL.

JR:	It's not a pretty picture, Danger. My father sacrificed himself to save the family name.
NICK:	And Bradshaw — the new D.A. — was gonna cover up for you and your dopey little operation here. But why did the General do it?
JR:	Don't waste any tears over my father. He was already dying of the incurable family disease.
NICK:	What's that? Terminal greed?
ROCKY:	No! Lead poisoning, Danger!
NICK:	Oh, no! Rococo!
JR:	(PULLING HIS PISTOL) Drop that gun!
ROCKY:	Huh? OK, boss. (HE DOES SO)
JR:	You idiot! (HE SHOOTS ROCKY)
ROCKY:	I'm dying! I'm dying . . . I'm dead! (HE DIES)
NICK:	You murdered him!
JR:	Don't waste any tears over poor cousin Ricky. Those Egyptian cigarettes were killing him anyway. Well, "Mr. Gomez," it looks like we have a Mexican standoff.

SUDDENLY, A SPOTLIGHT SHINES ON JUNIOR FROM ACROSS THE SEA. ANOTHER MOTOR IS HEARD, AND A VOICE AMPLIFIED BY BULLHORN:

BRAD: Ahoy, Perfect Alibi! This is the police! Prepare for boarding! We have you surrounded! Put up your hands!

NICK: That means you, Junior.

JR: Never! The family will never survive the scandal!

JUNIOR FIRES HIS PISTOL AT THE SPOTLIGHT. THE GUNFIRE IS RETURNED AND HE IS RIDDLED WITH BULLETS. HE MAKES HIS DYING SPEECH IN NICK'S ARMS:

JR: Don't waste any tears over me, Danger. I'm the last black sheep in a bad flock. There never was . . . a good . . . Starsucker . . .

THE TWO DEAD BODIES ROLL GENTLY BACK AND FORTH ON DECK AS LT. BRADSHAW COMES ON BOARD.

BRAD: Well! Looks like this makes me even with you, Danger.

NICK: The only thing even about you, Bradshaw, is the bottom of your flat feet. What're you talking about?

BRAD: Well, I tried to put ya in the hot seat, and now I pulled ya out of the fryin' pan. Ain't ya gonna thank me?

NICK: Yeah, Bradshaw. Thanks — for nothin'.

BRAD: Danger, lemme give ya a piece of advice . . . On second thought, I think I'll keep it to myself. Let's go, boys!

BRADSHAW DISEMBARKS, LEAVING NICK ALONE WITH THE BODIES. THEY ALL ROCK FOR A BEAT. THEN:

NICK: What a swell day. I lose my job, my car, my gun, my license, and almost lose my life. And what have I got left? A bullet-riddled boatload of magnolias and pain-killer. Well, things could be worse! I wonder how you steer one of these things — South . . .

NICK TAKES THE WHEEL AND STARTS TO TURN THE YACHT AROUND AS THE LIGHTS FADE TO A BLACKOUT. CLOSING FILM THEME MUSIC ENDS AND BECOMES A COOL JIVE THEME. THE LIGHTS COME UP ON THE JIVE CAT.

CAT: All right! It's late at night and you've got legal and dental problems. What you gonna do? You walk down to the corner of 179th and Seattle. It's terrifically BAD down there! There's Victor's House of Barbecued Bats on one corner and Ed's House of Threads on the other. But your teeth hurt and you got a sub-pena in your pocket! What you gonna do? You gotta go to Doctor Don Demographico's Twilight Sleep Clinic of Credit Law. Don's a graduate of the All-American School of Law — that's two tough years at UCLA law school, climaxed by two fun-filled weeks at the Costa Rican School of Dentistry! Family-proof dentures and taffy-proof wills are his specialty! No fee too large, no cavity too small. And, hey, sodium pentathal is available — and that's the truth! See ya . . .

THE LIGHTS FADE TO A BLACKOUT. WHEN THEY COME UP A TREMENDOUS RELIGIOUS MINISTRY IS UNDERWAY. JOEY IS THE MINISTER, "REVEREND DEE." HE IS JOINED BY TWIN MUSICIANS, "THE HAWK" AND "GIBBER" AND BY HIS GRAMPS IN HIS WHEELCHAIR.

JOEY: And these are the final hours of the final days, here on our All-Day, All-Night Hell City Hellathon! And it's up to you to put us over the edge! It's up to you to call me — Reverend Dee — and start lighting up those two thousand Princess telephones back there, or we're gonna go off the tube and down the tubes, dear friends! Let me read to you again from the same work I've been quoting to you from all night! From the subpoena, page 12, section 3, sub-paragraph 9: "We, the District Attorney, known herein as the people's complaints, and the aforementioned Trustees of the proposed receivership, do henceforth seize, squeeze and sequester the aforementioned moveable assets of the previously mentioned Shelter Corporation located in Hell City, etc., etc." In other words — they took my plane away! And all your computers were on that plane! And all your names were in those computers! And all our mailing lists! So, it's up to you, now. So where are you? You angels of Hell City, cornerstones of the Golden Pyramid, you Million Dollar Saints? Sell that extra car, that house you never use! If that hundred-dollar bill that's burning a hole in your pocket doesn't have my picture on it, send it to me! Because, my friends, there's much more at stake there than my TV family! This man here is much, much more than my dear grandfather, temporarily emotionally crippled by the Disgrace of God! This is the treasurer of our Corporation! And I'm the President! And Hawk and Gibber here are the Recordin' Secretaries! But they ain't gonna make any more recordin's unless those phones start lightin' up! They're gonna have police records! That's right! They want to put us in jail, 'cause jail is Hell, and nobody wants to go to Hell! But if we do, we want to go with a Hell of a lot more money than I see on that tote-board right now! Pay the Lord! So, come on Hell City Helpers! Join us in our never-ending battle against the monkey-brained motor-mouths sitting smugly in their centralized, soon-to-be-collapsing super-state! Join us in a song of salvation! That'll show 'em that we'll never let go! Join us in our Hell City Song of Sanity!

HAWK & GIBBER (SINGING):
As I walk through the shadow
Of the Valley of Debt,
I like to think of all the adults
And adulterers I have met.
As the cracklin' fire leaps up
From my feet down below,
I like to turn on my television set
And watch me on this show!

ALL (SINGING): I like to watch myself in the morning,
I like to watch myself instead of news!
And you can bet I'll watch myself in Heaven,
'Cause it's Hell down here in these shoes!

AS THEY SING, GRAMPS HAS A "MIRACLE CURE" AND DANCES BRIEFLY AROUND WITH THE OTHERS. THEN, AS THE OTHERS DEPART, HE COLLAPSES INTO HIS WHEELCHAIR AND STARES AT HIS TV SET.

CHAPTER 5: FROM BRECHT, VIA WILLIE THE SHAKE, TO JOEY'S HOUSE WE GO

THE MUSIC FADES. HE POKES AT THE CHANNEL CHANGER WITH HIS CANE.

GRAMPS: (AS A NEWSMAN) Finally, on the Too Late News, the Squid Alert continues in Southern California, right on down to the Mexican border. Scientists wonder . . . (HE FALLS ASLEEP)

DAD COMES IN, GIVES THE SLEEPING GRAMPS AN AFFECTIONATE PAT AND CHANGES THE CHANNEL, MOVING PAST SOME "WHITE NOISE" BETWEEN STATIONS.

DAD: Shhhhh . . . shhhhhh . . . "Lucy! Lucy! I'm home!"

DAD GOES INTO THE BATHROOM AND STARTS TO UNDRESS, THE "LUCY" SHOW CONTINUING AS MOM CHANGES CHANNELS TO THE STATION OF HER CHOICE:

MOM: (SHE'S A GUEST ON "TOMORROW") . . . You know, there's no real men any more in this country. Only guys with short hair and beards driving off-road vehicles up and down Rodeo Drive. There used to be a time when we had real men in this country — men like that great detective hero Nick Danger. Men who packed a rod and had a chest as big as all outdoors. Now, there's nothing . . .

MOM WANDERS OFF TO BED, TO JOIN DAD. JOEY COMES IN, READY TO LEAVE FOR WORK. HE CAN'T PASS BY THE TV, AND PICKS UP THE TV GUIDE.

JOEY: Hmmm. "Lucy's" over. This is "Women Late At Night." It's almost over. "Cheese Dances of Communist Spain" — nope, that's finished. I wonder if there's anything left . . . (CHANGING CHANNELS) Shhhhhhhh . . . Shhhhhhhh

HE CHANGES CHANNELS IN THE MIDST OF THE NATIONAL ANTHEM AND STOPS.

JOEY: Oh, boy! The jets'll be coming up soon! Great! Television — it never lets you down!

THE ANTHEM FINISHES AND THE LIGHTS FADE TO A BLACKOUT, LEAVING ONLY THE LIGHT FROM THE TV ON THE FACES OF JOEY AND GRAMPS. THEN FULL BLACKOUT AND THE CURTAIN FALLS.

THE END OF "JOEY'S HOUSE"

Monday 30 July — aft in S.B.
Over now. The review is in — I was "superb" — otherwise not such a rave.

Moving backward — Monday back into LA at 8 — our rehearsals from 10-3. Talked thru the piece Mon — Tues tried to get a run-thru — Wed had a runthru at noon — things moved slowly & I was personally not in much of a good mood abt things. The staging seemed promising, but I was in trouble on lines & nervous. My mood did improve, tho I felt really nervous abt the show, PA seemed slow & a bit hesitant abt getting into it. PB positive, PP more than usually nervous.

At the same time, biz was developing on the HBO project to the point that it seemed positive they might get John Ritter, which would have made the project "100%" — they may or may not get him — don't know yet.

Thurs we went over to the Roxy — same old place — for the show set, "set" painted, props and costumes in place, lights & sound set — it was 6 by the time we cld leave, go back to the Street & have a traditional crepe & pea soup dinner at Proctors'. Then back for the show, which was ragged & unrehearsed, but THERE. *A good response from the crowd. A middling to fair review but right insofar as it goes. I felt very nervous before the curtain, but did well anyway.*

The next few shows were all improvements, with 1st show Sat probably the best. Had sellouts Fri early & Sat early, then Sat late sold suddenly out. KTYD/Bozo bus people wonderful at Sat early show & we did our best for them. I felt very energized after & the late show went very well & the aud was hot. PA was slowest to come into focus — I don't know why — playing Mom seemed to be a real problem — but even Nick was blurred. He gained w/each perf, but seemed never to pull it all together perfectly. PP was mostly very good & very sharp Sat, with all the right props & mustaches & stuff. PB I really enjoyed, esp Bradshaw & the continuity of the Joey character.

I felt as if I had the easiest part, really — distinct characters & out of one whole sequence. (PP tried to write himself into Local H, but w/out success. PB was out of Nick 1.)

Of course home late after Sat show. Little party upstairs for PP's birthday — J. Benny's b'day! He very happy, in spite of my kneeing him in the balls when I died as Jr. S. — everyone very up — the shows good & the aud reaction very high — a half-standing ovation after the late Sat show.

I slept late this am. I went downtown & shopped & tried to get gas — no luck, or up to $1.02 for unleaded. They are doing the cummings play in LA today & tomorrow, with Ford Rainey as eec. That bodes well.

Actually, no. The recording of my cummings play went smoothly enough, but a few weeks later the producer called to say they were junking it and planning on re-recording with new actors. This never happened, and I sold the script to the BBC a year later.

At the same time, the HBO comedy, "The Madhouse of Dr. Fear," (50% old movie clips, script credited to Dean Christopher and Victoria Westermark, a Proctor-Bergman-Lockhart Production) went into rehearsal. The company included *Jeff the director who had not a funny idea in his head . . . All these people to do a really stupid half-hours worth of script. The rehearsal was simple-minded & I did all the work in staging my scenes and biz.* The next scheduled rehearsal was to be with John Ritter, the star (fresh from "Americathon"), but ABC was refusing to lend him to the project. The shoot dates were put off for a month.

NPR's Chris Koch, producer of "All Things Considered," called to ask if I could do an interview with Tim Leary (celebrated as "Tiny Dr. Tim" on Firesign's first album). Leary was appearing at the Improv.

Tues am 28 August
We went into LA Sun aft, had a bite, then on to the Ash Grove — sorry, the Improvisation — lots of folk there — M. Efron and H. Shearer (who is joining SNL next season — will it make him a star?), Rob Reiner also there — just the "young writers and directors" Tim Leary wanted in attendance.

TL himself — speedy, clear-eyed. He gave an illus. lecture, w/a few jokes — his pitch is Futurist — space colonies — thinks the 80s are going to be more exciting than the 60s, promotes hedonism. I thought he was both right — in his positive, up-beat view of The Future — & shallow in his "comedy." The int. went quickly & smoothly & was exciting. He said he'd tried to contact FT when in prison — ? — was glib — an accomplished personality.

As the Summer wore on in smoggy, hot, wild-fire-smoky Los Angeles, I found myself attending meetings with our "new partners" (I'll call them H&G) about a movie deal. Peter warned "don't try to impress them as young tycoons." As if we were.

I will go down w/out imposing my paranoia on "the established order." This time, he smiled.

I came home after mtg with H&G at CBS in Studio City — the 4 of us being TFT for their benefit — "getting to know you" blah — I wasn't really in the mood.

Did the commute again — this time it was hotter & smokier- went to Metro & the old HS — Thalberg Bldg — did a repeat performance w/Claire somebody — a VP at 27 — plus H&G, plus another guy, repping the presumed exec prod.

What DOES make Sammy run?

In mid-September NPR offered us a deal to cover the up-coming Presidential campaign — we were invited to do seven minutes a week on "Morning Edition" for the next year! *A real legit job at a good price. PB deserves congrats for his negotiating & I for my — what? — determination?* Plus our friends at Rhino Records agreed to put out an LP of the "Nick Danger" radio pilot we'd recorded back in January, so the work was not to be totally lost.

This goes a long way toward making 1980 a new year & decade — let the 70's fade on back now.

Many more commutes to LA as the 70's faded. In mid-October, with Phil Proctor suffering estrangement from his wife and only half-there, we had what I called *a 1968 sort of day — PA & PB talking. Me quiet. Good dope. Talk mostly of Men In Hats — lots of ideas — "Nick and Nancy Danger." Most enthusiasm right now going there.*

My marriage to Tinika was also strained, not helped by her getting a job at a new theatre company in Norfolk, Virginia, headed by an old friend from California, Patrick Tovatt. We decided to take the cross-country train to Washington DC. *Pomona, San Berdoo, Barstow. Up and breakfasted & then back to smoke a j. The black hostess tapped on our door & asked for one, it smelt so good! Smelled up the whole car. Recorded train sounds off the back. Next stop, Albuquerque.*

Three days later, in DC, I called Peter. *He was cheery as pie — UA PASSED (so goes the dream wld). No mention of H&G's pursuit of CBSTV — guess that went zzipping past. Shooting for HBO on next Friday the 2nd.* I had a fine meeting with NPR (it would only be a couple of years before I'd actually be working there) where I met tragically famous Frank Mankiewicz, the network's president and was offered a month as host of All Things Considered. (Mankiewicz was Robert Kennedy's press secretary when the Presidential candidate was assassinated, June 5, 1968.)

It was early November by the time the "Madhouse" shoot was finally scheduled. *Into makeup — mostly hair whitener & costume — good tail suit — "Bates." Very long slow day — shot one short scene early — the other at the end of the day.*

John Ritter had been replaced in "Madhouse" by Don Adams, who brought along his beloved shtick. *I was nervous 1st scene. Don Adams pleasant enough — odd to meet actor on set like that for the first time. I had my moment — topped Adams w/an ad lib & broke up the stage — left him behind closed door. I think the scenes went ok — I certainly was working broadly — but so does Adams. Won't know until I see footage.*

The next day Dr. Demento was premiering the 12-minute Nick Danger album over KMET. *Dr. Demento a small soft fellow — munchkiny — the one crazy record collector-type who rose to the top of the pail. I like him, but the show is awfully Jr. Hi School. We did good — our 13th anniv on radio — just abt. Everyone had a good time I think — lots of space allowed one another — beginnings of good improvs. Maybe the time will come again. The Nick Danger album sounds good too — I'd forgotten it entirely. That was our 1st project this year — out before year's end.*

"The Madhouse of Dr. Fear"

CHAPTER 6
MANY MEANWHILES

My 43rd year began with a cross-country drive, a VW bus breakdown in Odessa, Texas (first place on my "10 Cities Never to Visit Before You're Dead" list), New Years in football-mad Dallas, and a week in Washington D.C., meeting with a National Endowment for the Arts panel, judging grant applications for radio. It was pre-metal-detector-time and the Capitol was as it should be for everyone — free and open.

NPR's new program, "Morning Edition," was offering Firesign a home and the independent radio movement was creating a new and exciting form of radio theatre (often credited to our influence). It was fascinating to be a part of this initial creative process of young National Public Radio. We worked steadily on our "Campaign Chronicles," the pieces mostly individually written and then improvised on by the group when we met in LA to record with our favorite studio producer, Fred Jones.

World politics heading into the election year 1980 were in the dumper. The 53 Americans taken hostage back in November were still hostages. The Soviets had invaded Afghanistan on Christmas Eve. The early days of January 1980 found the President bailing out Chrysler to the tune of a billion-and-a-half and Teddy Kennedy announcing he'd run against Carter, giving the Firesign another candidate to profile.

So far, we had only Jerry Brown, even then Governor of California, for the Dems and a passel of the usual names (George Bush the elder, Howard Baker, Bob Dole) all running hindmost to Ronald Reagan. Those of us who didn't much like Carter and had good reason to fear Reagan had John Anderson, a quirky Republican "moderate" from Illinois who ran as an independent after Reagan conquered the nomination.

In addition, Phil Austin created a brilliant parody of Reagan — Daffy Duck, the come-back movie star totally out of control! Wa-hoo! Wa-hoo! And Phil Proctor came up with "President" Woppler, pronounced "wop-pleer," who had changed his first name to "President" and urged using cats to deliver the mail because of their "wonderful sense of direction." Even the former Vice Presidential candidate of the Nat'l Surrealist Party ticket returned for some outspoken editorials:

GEORGE TIREBITER COMMENTARY — IT'S TOO SPOOKY

You know, with the present attempt to rehabilitate the "spooks" going on in Congress and former Company leader George Bush burning for the GOP nomination, it's time to stop letting these slippery dogs lie.

As I see it, Bush's protestations to the contrary, spying is a fifth-rate, pulp novelist's damp-sheeted fantasy — the appeal of which speaks to that "I'm just naturally better than you are" prep school mentality still archly maintained by this supposedly "distinguished public servant" and Presidential candidate.

Let's face it, in the Animal House of fat-boy fraternities the undercover life must seem pretty appealing — all those swell suits, phones in suitcases, a warm spot near the Seat of Power.

But we know all this CIA business adds up to just one thing — they put your tax money in the pockets of dishonest and disreputable princes and politicians whose loyalties extend as far as the nearest bank vault.

So come on, George Bush — being in the intelligence agency doesn't make you intelligent — just another smart cookie, preserved on the federal payroll, your soft secrets buried like nuts and raisins under the sugary dough.

This is George Tirebiter for National Public Radio.

"Campaign Chronicles" began running two mornings a week on November 14, 1979. Many pieces (there were two or three elements in each four-minute segment) were tied to news events, but the general tone became more and more surreal as the writing progressed, alongside the creation of the "Fighting Clowns" Roxy show. The politics of the Chronicles influenced the writing of the stage show and, a couple of months later, of the album version. And all sorts of people showed up!

KISSINGER COMMERCIAL SPOT

Hello! I'm so loveable and popular I might as well be Henry Kissinger, and I'm extraordinarily proud of myself again for getting paid to offer you "Henry's Years — The 1970s in Butter Dishes." Ya wol! Ten priceless affordable butter-plates from the Imperial Collection by Rockyfellow of

5th Avenue. A perfect frame for your collection of Presidential Portraits in Butter.

Just listen to what they look like — a beautiful Persian-style design in pure fool's gold depicting each of the Ten Super-Historic Events of the Decade — hand-painted by talented Cambodian expatriates.

Start your collection now with Plate Number One: "1973 — The POWs Come Home!"

Plus, if you send the usual amount to the usual place, my people will include a copy of my latest doorstop, now available in paperback for lightweights, like you!!!

Remember, that's "Henry's Years — The 1970s in Butter Dishes." Why not order by phone? We'll be listening!

Special reports flooded into Firesign News Central:

I RAN — FOR PRESIDENT! AMERICA HELD HOSTAGE BY ITS OWN GOVERNMENT, WEEK TWO

Events in the little country of Iran-For-President moved quickly last week as the Ayatolyallso Jimmicarter addressed his countrymen from the holy city of GWashington in the sternest terms. Rejecting the course of his predecessor, the hated and deposed Imperial Presidency, Jimmicarter firmly imposed his conservative religious doctrine of hard-shell, born-again paternalism.

Quoting the great profit Mobiloil, the Ayatolyallso said, "We will cut off the noses of our children, in spite of what they face! Women are as equal in death as in Life, Time and People!" The Superbowl Powers remained in formation, ready to move from defense to offence to preserve the Straits of Exxon and the Gulf of Oil from an all-out blitz.

Opposition to the Ayatolyallso has altered considerably in the past few days. Some opponents have sustained serious injuries in the struggle to move to Jimmicarter's right, a crowded spot, where everybody's back is up against the wall.

So far, little has been heard from the Ayatolyallso's left-wing opposition, Edward Le Kennedi, at least not by this reporter, banned like all correspondents from the Rose Garden, and awaiting a cable from Kabul.

This has been a Firesign Special Report.

And, of course, the Sports Networks were as political as any other news source, as in this sketch by Phil Austin:

THE DESERT GOLF-RAT SHOOT

ED: And welcome back to the thirty-fifth annual Palm Springs Desert Golf-Rat Shoot. The surprise today, as we look at the leader board, is the sudden surge of Presidential candidates among the front-runners in the celebrity ranks. For a report, at the ninth tee is Jack Rodenticus. Jack?

JACK: At the ninth tee is Ted Kennedy, sporting a thin, elegant mustache that makes him look very much like David Niven. His partner, Lee Trevino has just hit a beautiful wood shot to the green. Here's Kennedy with that preppy backswing — the shot is hooking — over the bridge and, oh, oh, into the water. Kennedy's in trouble now. He'll have to dive for that ball — he's talking it over with family and friends and it looks like — yes, he will dive for the ball now and call the police in the morning. Ed?

ED: That definitely might throw Kennedy out of the hunt. Here's Sam Norvegicus at the sixteenth —

SAM: Ed, a big rat has poked its head out of a tumbleweed just three feet from where Ronald Reagan's chip shot lies for a possible birdie here on the tough sixteenth. Reagan has called for a double-O-gauge shotgun from his caddie. Rather unusual choice here. Most pros would choose to go after the rat with a knife, but Reagan has played in this tournament for years and . . .
(BLAM!)
Uh oh! Looks like he overshot — and hit his ball! The course officials will have some rule-making to do here, since I can't remember this ever happening before. Ed?

ED: You're right, Sam. It never has happened before. By the way, those bright green pants that the rat is wearing were designed by Hubert Green and all the rats working the course today . . . wait a minute — let's go down to Jackie Stewart on the seventeenth . . .

JACKIE:	Ed, there's a terrible problem developing here. Janet Guthrie, the lady race driver, has freaked out after her ball was cannibalized by two rats using an acetylene torch and tiny hi-speed golf carts. Right behind her on the course is President Jimmy Carter trying to take his tee shot, and he'll have to take it on a dogleg right around this screaming, hysterical woman. This is the first time the President has set foot outside the White House since the many international crises that have dominated his attention — except, of course, for short, supervised trips to the bathroom — and this can't be helping his already limited attention span. No, he's not going to play the shot. That's right! He's walking away from the tee . . . Oh! Would you look at that! What a move! He's smashed a rat that was hiding behind a spectator — smashed it flat! This will certainly move him up . . . I'm just getting word that Kennedy has shot an eagle on the ninth, but he used a fully-automatic AR-round. This will get him in trouble with environmentalists . . . so let's go to Ben Bland on the eighteenth . . .
BEN:	Ed, it's bad here. A fistfight has broken out between Anderson, Brown and Bush over scorecards. Jerry Brown has flattened the other two with two round-house rights, but only succeeded in allowing three of his captured rats to get loose from the three-piece suit he was using to confine them. The rats have taken over choice seats at the clubhouse bar and are telling all Reagan's jokes in advance to spectators. This could hurt . . .
ED:	Sorry to cut in, Ben, but that's all the time we have now. We'll be back tomorrow for the final round of the Palm Springs Desert Golf-Rat Shoot, but now let's join Jim McKay at the Disgruntled Alternate Olympic Site in Plains, Georgia. Jim?

Well, sports news runs 24/7, so we'll just cut away. When Christmas '79 rolled around, most candidates were included in a medley of carols. John Connolly got "O Tannenbaum:"

Oh, Connolly, "Tex" Connolly,
I'll drink to you and Lyndon B.
Your hair is gray, you've got the look,
Your suit is dap, you're not a crook.
But Connolly, poor Connolly,
I'm here to say you're Number Three!

At that point, it was impossible to remember all the jobs that two lesser candidates had held in their decades in government. We gave Howard Baker and George Bush "Jingle Bells:"

Baker/Bush, Baker/Bush
One's the CIA
The other is a millionaire
But we don't care which way — oh!
Baker/Bush, Baker/Bush
One's a Senator
The other is a bureaucrat
But we don't know what for — oh!
Dashing to and fro
In New Hampshire snow
Oh, who cares if one's a spy
They both will go away — hey!

We saved our big musical numbers for the forthcoming Roxy gig — songs for Reagan, Ford, Carter and Jerry Brown were part of a political set for The Eight Shoes, our Vegas-style lounge act booked into the Roxy wearing their powder-blue tuxedos.

THE ROXY SHOW

In January, LA was good and wet from heavy rain when I got back from DC and the NEA radio grants panel. *An excellent panel*, one of whose members was Denise Oliver-Velez, a Black Panther Party activist and program director at WPFW, Pacifica's new DC station. A very tricky process, this grant-giving.

Friday aft — 18 Jan 80
Finally a clear day. It's rained all week, more or less. Monday went to Blues Concert — Big Mama Thornton & Cleanhead Vinson — enjoyable. Tues into LA for a long day — mostly discussion of radio plans and talking about a Roxy date. Some enthusiasm, but we broke up on a note of uncertainty. PB frustrated (w/me) abt not being a TV star — just that PB crazyness bubbling up — but we had a good recording session and PB & I talked while P's mixed a song, & the excitement returned. I called PA Wed am to get him to call Lanny, & we got our Leap Year date! Fast going.

Now what?

Thurs down to LA — another rainy day at PB's — mostly a day on wld politics — PP quiet, w/a cold. PA in really good shape & PB kicking in his quarter.

A few days later, I was back in LA, this time staying in "The Studio", Peter's girlfriend's apartment on Hyperion Blvd. Tinika was in Virginia and it was very lonely in Los Angeles.

Day started w/PP presenting treatments of a P&B script — he frust that TFT didn't have anything written to present at H'wood mtgs — well, me too!

Anyway — good long day of discussion in which ev tried to clarify feelings. I sd that I saw "TFT Film" as distinct from a "REAL FILM." PP really wanted to do real film. PB at that moment hot on their last riff — var on HCYB — PA trying to put it all together —

Suddenly the ideas of x-country trip (by "Babe" char) mated w/ "Homer's Odyssey" — the obvious struck — PP wanted to call it "I Think We're All — etc" — & I heard the elements clicking together in place. PA ecstatic. Smooth transition to rest of day on Roxy Show — plugging away at the comic ideas & seeing what works & what can be extended.

The next day, January 25th, was cold and cloudy. The end of a break in the steady winter rains.

We split our time between a reading of the Odyssey and work on the "Bozos (Homer's

Odyssey)" film treatment, and more work on the Roxy '80 show. Spirits much higher than when the week began on Tues & the quick progress delighted everyone.

Drove in Fri — 3 trips in 24 hours is really wearing — but another good long day — wrote a bunch of candidate's songs (interrupted by a call fr a fan in NJ) songs — yes, the beg of "The Invasion of Afghanistan" & more — busy day — oh, yes — song "We're All Bozos on this Bus — This Bus is Off to War!"

Really good day — in spite of my persistent anger — directed towards PB — about current war talk — PB defending Carter & char. the Ruskies as "evil" which is imp. for me to buy. Odd how heavy the tensions are — the '80s — what a bomb!

Thurs 31 Jan
Mon & Tues in LA — drove in Mon & it was dry here, but rained all the way in from the Rincon. Met at the studio — long day on Mon — still song-writing & rehearsing — did a lot of singing & had a good time.

Wet but not raining Tues — had a slow am by myself — didn't go out to eat — then the day's mtg — wrote "Love Agent Orange" and worked hard.

Monday February 11th marked 100 days of captivity for the American hostages in Iran and we were turning the news into a play with music we were calling "Meanwhile." The previous Friday *was another intense workday . . . In the pushing and pulling PP confused but improving — his "little joke" was to keep suggesting we do the last show — just a real horror of new writing — brain fatigue, I'd say. PB slow to deliver — PA pleading for spontaneity & just following what comes — his style. & I worked hard to encourage what ultimately came out as The Towel Play.*

After a weekend home in Santa Barbara, I drove back down to smoggy LA. *Another day of hard work — finished "Meanwhile" and took care of a misc of other business, also sang some. Tues we began early — 10:30 and worked steadily until 4 — wrote "Bill" based on PA's reggae idea, & new verses for the Brown Blues & Carter song. Virtually done w/the script now — music rehearsal Fri & last writing day (+ interview) on Saturday.*

The rain continued. Phil Austin called to say his house was leaking. One storm followed another and on Saturday there was a *slow, steady downpour . . . This new storm arrived sometime in the night & looks as if it might continue indefinitely.*

I wasn't feeling terribly sentimental about The Firesign Theatre at that moment. Phil Proctor seemed to lack any enthusiasm for the material we were a couple of weeks from premiering. *His anger level is way up.*

Peter was worried about money. He's trying to be modest — but he is always on the edge — the TV pilot thing surfaces as something that cld solve his $ dilemma, yet (as he insisted yest) he doesn't want TFT to become the focus of his needs. PA is really being sweet as pie.

I got a bit feisty at PB yest & felt bad abt it — not really so irritated w/him as w/the group — its cheapness, its lethargy, its lack of corporate ambition, its unwillingness to struggle or work cheap & strive high. We are certainly politically divided — but we've been that before — notably in the election year '72.

Truly, at the moment I'm more excited abt my own future than TFT's — because who can say what that future might be?

It needs focus, direction & a clear understanding among us about what we intend to do following The Roxy.

No matter about the Future, on February 18th 1980 it was still raining in Los Angeles. It was a Southern California monsoon. It rained hardest, inches more, at the tops of the Hollywood Hills. The canyons became rivers. The intensity of the rain virtually shut LA down. Both Phils had water running through their houses. Proctor was close to hysteria trying to locate a "water vacuum" while we had a soggy interview with the LA Times. Austin left to bail out his garage. Peter and I finished the interview and I tried to take him home to his new place in Benedict Canyon.

Big mistake! We came from Mulholland Drive at the crest of the Hollywood Hills down a steep street called Deep Canyon. The water was running down the road faster than we were driving. Deep Canyon ends at another narrow canyon street called Hutton. I stopped. We looked. Hutton was a raging river. OK, I thought, Pete doesn't live too far down the river, maybe I can make it. At the last minute, before we were washed miles south to Sunset Boulevard, a huge machine loomed out of the rain and mist like an apparatus from "Star Wars," churning up waves. A voice hailed us: "Go back! Go back!" I muscled the car around and we sailed back upstream to Mulholland and contemplated our next move. The Valley — the San Fernando Valley of pop song fame — stretched invisibly north in the fog from the foot of these hills. Peter suggested a friend — one Ralph Burris — who had a home not far away in Encino. We made it there through flooded streets.

Had a wonderful serendipitous evening — the rain poured w/incredible ferocity — Ralph showed us the TRS-80 & we spent the rest of the evening playing a marvelous game like D&D — requiring great brain exercise & establishing rapport w/a great program.

That evening with one of the earliest home computers gave us the electronic germ of our next album project — "The Pink Hotel Burns Down." The rain stopped briefly, *but abandoned cars lined the freeway & there were slides & mud & flooding everywhere.* On Monday the 101 was closed in a couple of places northbound, but lucky me, clear into LA. We had a music rehearsal with Richard Parker. The rain began again and *eventually the Phils had to go home to their flooded houses.* Our opening at The Roxy was a week away.

It's raining again ——— in more ways than one.

A TV "offer" had come our way. Nothing real of course, but demanding of our divided attention. Proctor insisted we make a yes or no decision on a deal which would have us be "comic actors" in somebody else's script. He thought it would be a great idea and Peter joined in. Professionally, it seemed not in our interests. We were known as writers as well as actors, and the writing was what it was all about for me. *To me it's all Twinkies.*

There was one of those "Well, that's it" sort of dramatic sighs from P&B. Then, to my astonishment PB said that he was "disappointed" & that he would now have to decide how much of his life he could devote to FT & how much to pursuing this new goal of being a TV star. Not a great deal went down after that — I was totally discouraged — to have our goals be so different, to be made the spoiler — the only hitch between "failure & success" — to have such anger from PB — over SHIT — well — I barely made it thru a very unfunny photo session for the Times & a desultory rewrite of "Billville."

I got out as fast as I could at 4 & drove home in a downpour — past the flooded strawberry fields in Camarillo, slides on the coast — the huge muddy waves at the Rincon — & home — sound and secure . . .

Monday night — 25 February 80
First day of rehearsal of the final week — it's coming down to it now.

Drove in Friday for writing session — beginning atmos was cool, but the day went well & gradually things got better. We rolled the rug up & rehearsed in the living room & did the 2nd rewrite on Billville.

Sat am went out to the Valley & spent the day singing w/the band — the mood of the week lifted.

Yesterday — Monday — drove in to the Roxy early — spent the day there rehearsing — ate lunch across the street & said hello to Steve Martin — Parker came in aft to work out accompaniment to sketches.

We rehearsed music and sketches for long days at the Roxy and our studio producer, Fred Jones, surprised us with a record contract with Mushroom, an Australian label, which allowed us to record (24-track) all the Roxy performances and produce an album. Other looming issues were put aside for the moment.

Fri aft — 29th Feb 80
Two blurred days — Wed was an all-day rehearsal — I went out to eat at Norm's — what a freak show that is — unfailingly a great place, then on to the Roxy to study lines in the car & walk the stage. No music, we just worked the sketches — I had terrible line problems w/"Billville" that hung me up until the actual show.

Thurs — out early to get coffee at Norm's — very "up" & nervous abt the show — went on to the Roxy — we got a music rehearsal, ran "Meanwhile," got a 15-minute light rehearsal & waited hours for the show (9 pm). But atmosphere was good — a nice first crowd & a small but responsive 2nd house.

The first show was ruff — PP blew a lot of lines — I had my long scene pretty well but blew some other lines.

Did a bit of revision between shows, but basically just cooled off. Enjoyed the second show very much. Stayed late to say hello to people (Harry Shearer there & it was very nice to see him). Home really tired & tried to stay in bed but up & out by 11 for b'fast at Norm's & to read the review — a pretty good one from Gardener McKay in the H-Ex.

FRI — we made a couple of changes in the show — a minimum of tiny cuts & included "This Bus Is Back From War" in the Fuddz set, which gave the show an ending — almost.

The Friday night audience was very hot & the shows were tiring, but I wasn't very nervous abt them, just winded and sweaty afterwards. Big celeb by Mushroom — photos & champagne in the interval & much corporate enthusiasm. Stella Stevens was this year's celebrity guest.

Sat shows almost up to Friday — we were calmer & more together, lights were better. Audience just a bit cooler, but still very nice & we did get good, almost standing ovations.

The next Thursday we brought the show north to the Lobero Theater in Santa Barbara. The Lobero is an old house and we were delighted to think we were treading the boards the Marx Bros. had trod when they were working up their early films in front of a live audience.

The first show was very satisfying — the 2nd had a hotter aud & gave us a standing ovation. We gave good shows — good singing & some wonderful ad libs. Show sold 500 tx between noon & late show, so houses were full and we made some money too.

The pieces that went into building the Roxy Show, finally titled "Meanwhile In Billville — A Full Frontal Entertainment," were a combination of songs, performed by The Eight Shoes — a Rat Packaged club act, and by the punk group Fuddz, with comedy by The Fighting Clowns of Hollywood, all being performed in the nightclub at The Roxy Hotel in Ragbul, a "Casablanca" or "Camino Real" sort of joint.

The Muzbag National Opera Company was there with "Meanwhile, or the Invasion of Afghanistan, A Traditional Turkish Towel Play." Towels made for simple costumes.

The El Teatro Tabula Raza Guerilla Theatre Ensemble unveiled "Billville, or Destroying the Cities In Order To Save Them." (Billville, somewhere in the middle of fly-over America, was rediscovered in 1999 for Firesign's "Boom Dot Bust" CD.)

The Eight Shoes presented a "Tribute to American Politics" for their set. Fuddz closed the show with a couple of tunes from their black & white EP, "Sausages With Eyes."

Here's a bit of dialog that never made it into the show, but it does help explain who these clowns were:

DO:	Hello, I'm Mort.
PA:	Hello, I'm Hungry.
PB:	Hello, I'm War.
PP:	And sometimes I'm Happy — Hi!
ALL:	We're The Fighting Clowns!
PB:	Guess what?
ALL:	What?
DO:	Why did the chicken cross the road?
PA:	To make reality less painful!
PB:	Well, Mr. Smiths, I don't know about you, but I'm going to the Club.
PA/PP:	Why, Mr. Smith? To make reality less painful?
PB:	No, I'm just going to cross the road and eat the chicken on the other side!

The "Fighting Clowns" that emerged in the Roxy production and became the title act of the record album were reminders of the Brechtian origins of the show. One possible introduction came right out of "The Three Penny Opera":

> You are now going to hear a few songs from an Opera For Clowns. This Opera is called "Fighting Clowns" because things are so bad that Clowns must serve as soldiers in the Cold War Against The State. First, you will hear a ballad about the Evil Empire, called "The Bozos Song."

Another concept toyed with a different title:

> You are about to hear a full-frontal entertainment for Sausages. Since this entertainment was conceived with a splendor only a Sausage could imagine, and since it had to be so cheap even a Sausage could afford to see it, it is called "Sausages With Eyes."

When we rearranged the order of scenes and songs for the album, we returned to the earliest ideas we'd had for the live show: a 3-Ring Circus, a USO Bozo Tent Show, a Carnival Barker:

BARKER: Pssssst!

BOZO: Huh?

BARKER: Yeah, hey, come on! Get inside quick! The show just started!

BOZO: Show? No . . . What does it cost?

BARKER: Who cares? It'll make Reality less painful!

BOZO: Great balls of fire!

BARKER: Come on! Hurry up! Get in! (CALLS) Chair for Mr. Smith! (TO BOZOS) Hey, boys! Come over here quick! Come on!

BOZOS: Huh? What?

BARKER: Get inside — the show's about to start!

BOZO 2: Oh, no. We're broke.

BOZO 3:	Yeah! The inflation, you know. It's terrible.
BOZO 2:	How much does it cost?
BARKER:	Don't worry boys, you paid for it already! Hurry up! Get inside!
BOZOS:	Well, gee . . . OK . . .
BARKER:	(CALLS) Two more chairs for two more Smiths!
BOZOS:	Let's go . . .
BARKER:	This way for the recruiting show! Step up for the recruiting show! (HE FADES OFF)
CLUB M.C.:	Ladies and gentlemen! On the center stage, the Canteen is happy to present "The Fighting Clowns!"

The Roxy show opened with The Fighting Clowns already at War — on their computer screens, egged on by the Ringmaster (or is he the Ringlieder?) . . .

WE'RE ALL BOZOS ON THIS BUS

Bozos, Beaners, Zips, Berserkers,
Coupon-clippers, factory workers,
Old folks hiding in the attic,
Mothers, truckers, dope fanatics!

RINGMASTER: They're here tonight.
Everybody's here tonight!

Patriotic Rooski haters,
Punk platoons of roller skaters,
Child molesters, nuke protesters,
All will go to War! Hey!

RINGMASTER: Hey, hey, hey, hey! Are you ready for it, huh? You ready to sacrifice everything for "The Cause," because...? Hummm? Are you ready? You're all smiling now, but will you be smiling, say, six months from now? Are you really ready to give up your gas and your precious pocket calculators? Hmmmm? Ha ha ha! We'll see!

No more eating TV Dinners!
No more being Game Show Winners!
No more playing Craps and Faro!
No more driving your Camaros!

Camaro! Camaro! There'll be no more Camaros...

RINGMASTER: Errrrrrrkkkk... Watch out for that Pinto! Crrrrrraaaaaaassssssshhhhhh! Land o' Goshen!

Bozos, Beaners, Zips, Berserkers,
Aborted, pregnant welfare workers,
We're all Bozos on this Bus!
This Bus is off to War! Hey!

RINGMASTER: Oh, yes, yes, yes! You're all cheering now, aren't you, huh? But I wonder if that smile on your face isn't really a Cheshire smile, eh? Painted on! Yes, I can see your real faces! Yes, yes! I can see some people over there who look like live-in-lover beaters. Yes, yes! And there's a whole section of Lotos Eaters. And in the middle there, a whole bunch of tax-form cheaters, eh? But listen carefully to what we have to say...

I met a funny, bearded fellow
From the Gulag Archipelago-oh-oh . . .
Oh! They let him go!

RINGMASTER: Das vidanya, tovarich!

They said the Russian Bear was mean!
Let's wipe them off our TV screen!
Let's practice being Soviet shooters
On our family game computers!
Rooski POW!
Ruski POW!

(ALTERNATE VERSE)
He said the Eagle's lost his scream.
They'll wipe us off their radar screens!
They'll practice shooting Uncle Sammy
With their neutron double-whammy!

RINGMASTER: Yes, that's right! It's time again to play that wonderful game you can play at home on your own TV screen — "Rooski POW!" Let's see what kind of sharp-shooters we have out there today. Ah, you, young lady! How'd you like to try and stop that Soviet soldier before he stops you? Just say "Rooski POW!" and see if you can get him:

LADY: Rooski POW!

RINGMASTER: Uh oh! He's still heading toward the Club!
Try again!

LADY: Rooski POW!

RINGMASTER: Hey! We stopped him! Ha ha ha ha!
(We're only playing, folks!)

Bozos, Beaners, Zips, Berserkers!
Heroes, zeros, closet jerkers!
We're all Bozos on this Bus,
The President's is driving us,
Not one of us will make a fuss.
This bus is off to War!

(ALTERNATE VERSE)
But some of us have made a fuss!

(You ought to hear that Christian cuss,
'Cause all of us won't fight the Russ!)
This Bus won't go to War!

MEANWHILE IN BILLVILLE, or
Destroying The Cities In Order To Save Them

A Revolutionary Interpretation of the Militant
Socialist Vaudeville Play,
Re-translated by the El Teatro Tabula Raza Theatre
Ensemble from "Liberating the City of Woos," as
adapted from the Chinese by Ernest Umlaut

*

A CARD IS REVEALED WHICH READS:
"BILLVILLE"

MAYOR PENISNOSE APPEARS IN HIS OFFICE

MAYOR

Welcome to Billville. I'm the Mayor. This is my luxurious office, paid for by you citizens of Billville — that's you, Bill, and you, Bill, and you, Bill. You paid the bill. This is my phone. Ring, ring, ring. My secretary gets it and tells them to wait a minute, please. Buzzes me — buzz, buzz. Hello. Tells me it's Dinklebeek, President of the Billville City Council. Asks me if I want to put him on hold. Say, no, just put him on. Click. Hello, Dinklebeek, Mayor Penisnose here. *(He always pronounces it "P'NIS-NOZAY")*

What? The garbagemen are on strike? They're going to lose their homes? Let 'em sleep in the police cars. What about the cops? Let 'em put out the fires. What about the firemen? Let 'em eat the garbage. You work it out and don't quote me or I'll have you kneecapped. Ring, ring. Oh, oh, someone on the other line. Gotta go take a bribe. I mean, place a bet. Disconnect, click click. I wanna put fifty big ones on — hey, who is this? Mrs. Grundy of the Board of Education. Oh, yeah — well, me too! Don't you get it you old bag? I'm bored of education, too. Well, what is it? The schools are going to open! After all I've done. Are you crazy? We can't gas the busses. No, we can't gas the children. I've got it! Gas the teachers and we can use the school grounds for the Alternate Olympics. You work it out and don't quote me or I'll put your tits in a wringer. Disconnect. Dial tone. I hang up. Phone rings again. Ring ring ring ring. Secretary's out to lunch. Ring ring ring ring. Picks up phone himself.

THE DOCTOR APPEARS IN HIS OFFICE

DOC

Mayor Penisnose.

MAYOR

Penisnose!

DOC

Yeah, who cares. Look, this is Infermo at City Health. We're in big trouble. Big trouble!

MAYOR

Big, big, big! That's the spirit.

DOC
Shut up. Listen, the wells are poisoned.

MAYOR
Of course they're poisoned. You poisoned them.

DOC
But you told me to.

MAYOR
That's because I'm the Mayor.

DOC
Mayor Penisnose?

MAYOR
Penisnose! Who is this?

DOC
This is Infermo at City Health.

MAYOR
Ah! Doctor Infermo. Wasn't I just talking to you?

DOC
I don't remember. My mind has been going. I think it's because of the water. Did you hear? The wells have been poisoned.

MAYOR
They have?

DOC
You see? You've forgotten too.

MAYOR
Forgotten what? Who is this?

DOC
Who's this?

MAYOR
Mayor Penisnose.

DOC

Ah, Penisnose.

MAYOR

Penisnose! I'm putting you on hold.

DOC

Oh, no you don . . .

MAYOR

Click. I'm calling my bookie. Push, push, push, push, push, push, push.

THE COACH APPEARS ON THE FIELD

COACH

Ring, ring. Great time, boys! Ring, ring. God damn it! Say now, y'all go do another hunert laps and drink 'bout fifty gallons of milk. It'll make you big, big, big. Ring, ring. Coach Bill B. Dad here, Billville Atheletic Department. Say, are you an atheletic supporter?

MAYOR

Very jocular.

COACH

"Jockular!" Hee, hee! God damn!

MAYOR

I wanna place a bet.

COACH

Say! It must be Mayor Bill! Well, awrite! What's the action?

MAYOR

I wanna bet the entire Billville Crippled Widows and Destitute Orphans Pension Plan on the Billville team to take one-hundred big gold ones at our Alternate Olympics. How does it look?

COACH

Big, big, big!

MAYOR

Good, good, good. Remember, Coach. Ninety-nine-and-a-half gold medals just won't do. It's a hundred gold medals or I'll lose the bet and Billville will be taken over. It's in the bag?

COACH
Better yet, it's in the milk.

DOC
It's in the water, too.

ALL THREE HANG UP THEIR PHONES AND LEAVE

BILLY APPEARS AT HOME, DRINKING AND SMOKING

BILLY
(*Singing*) I'm a pepper! He's a pepper! You're a pepper! Wouldn't you like to be a pecker too? Coke adds life and everybody needs a little death. Bubble bubble bubble. The Pepsi de-de-de-Generation coming at you huge and long. So when it's time to relax, one thing is clear. I'm tired of pop. I want some Billy Beer!

COACH DAD ENTERS THE HOME

COACH
Oh, Billy Billy Billy Billy Billy!

BILLY
Why don't you call me Bill for short?

COACH
I will because you are, Bill. You're still too small. You're not big, big, big.

BILLY
But, Dad . . .

COACH
Call me Coach, son.

BILLY
Yes, sir.

COACH
That's better. You terrify me, boy.

BILLY
I do?

COACH
I'm scared for you, Bill. I'm worried about you, Bill. Deeply, truthfully, sincerely worried about you, Bill.

BILLY
What did I do?

COACH
It ain't what you did. It's what you didn't do. Assume the position, Bill.

BILLY
OK, Coach.

COACH
It's too small.

BILLY
It was real big when I woke up this morning.

COACH
I'm talkin' about your neck, Billy.

BILLY
My neck? What's wrong with my neck?

COACH
Pump it up! This isn't a world-class neck, Bill.

BILLY
What do you want me to do?

COACH
Hell! Stand up and lift up both your legs.

BILLY
Both of them?

COACH
How many you got?

BILLY
Anything you say, Coach. (*He falls to the floor.*) I fall down.

COACH
See, you pathetic creature? Your legs won't even support you. They're not big enough. World-class legs have got to be THIS big! That's big big big!

BILLY
Why, why, why?

COACH
Because of the Alternate Free World Olympics right here at Billville High. That's why. Get up.

BILLY
Yes, Coach.

COACH
Call me Dad. I'm in your corner.

BILLY
Yeah. I feel cornered too.

COACH
Every man, woman and person between the ages of eighteen and twenty has gotta go for the gold for Billville. Ain't that right?

BILLY
Heck, yes, Coach.

COACH
HELL, yes, boy!

BILLY
You said the "H" word.

COACH
Are you gonna slalom down Mt. Billy on that neck, son, and win us one of them hundred gold medals?

BILLY
But, Coach — I didn't qualify for the neck-skiing team.

COACH
Well, you will if you drink your goddam fuckin' milk!

BILLY
You said the "G&D" word and the "F" word, Coach. You're going to teach me the whole alphabet!

COACH
Sheeee . . . !

BILLY
That's the "S" word!

COACH
Listen, Billy . . .

BILLY
Listen to what, Coach?

COACH
Listen to me and tell me why you won't drink your goddam milk?

BILLY
(*He has trouble getting it out*) I can't drink my — my — my — my . . .

COACH
(*He keeps interrupting*) Come on, Billy . . . Don't be afraid to tell me . . . Why can't you . . .

BILLY
I'm afraid of it.

COACH
Afraid of what?

BILLY
I don't remember.

COACH
Must be the water.

BILLY
No, it's the milk. I'm afraid of my milk!

COACH
What a catastrastroke! My God, he's either got emotional sickness or worms in his glands!

BILLY

Gland-worms?

COACH

I'm so upset I don't know what to do.

BILLY

(*Singing*) When it's time to relax . . .

COACH

That's it. I could get drunk.

BILLY

But you are drunk, Dad.

COACH

That's right. Then let's slalom down and see Doctor Infermo at the Billville Health Center.

THE DOCTOR APPEARS IN HIS OFFICE

DOCTOR

Ring ring. Where's my secretary? Ring ring ring. Collapsed in the drug cabinet. Picks up. Doctor Infermo, Billville City Health. I know the wells are poisoned. I know it's a catastrophe, that's why I'm offering a special on catastrophic health insurance. No, huh? Well, how about a catastrophic illness? Oh, you've got one — it's in the water. Well, how about an autopsy? Half price. See you in the alley at two. You bring the coathanger. Hangs up.

COACH

Knock knock knock.

DOC

I didn't say that. Who's there?

COACH

Big Coach Bill Dad.

DOC

Hell, no!

COACH

Hell, yes!

DOC

Bust down the door!

COACH AND BILLY ENTER AS CHEERLEADERS

COACH & DOC

(*A cheer*) Big Big Big! Bill Bill Bill! Billlllll-villlle!

BILLY

The Big One.

DOC

Who's this wimp?

COACH

He's a left-over from one a' my first three marriages.

DOC

What's wrong with his neck? It's so small small small.

COACH

He says he's afraid of his milk.

THE DOC, OVERREACTING, PERFORMS A RITUAL WITCH-DOCTOR CEREMONY

DOC

He must be nuts. Are there Martians in the milk, Billy?

BILLY

I didn't see any.

DOC

Well, we're not afraid of drinking, are we? We dwink our widdle Coca-Cola, don't we?

BILLY

Yeah, but it makes my teeth swell and the Gatorade makes my pee green.

DOC

That's the color of peas, isn't it? What's wrong with that?

COACH

Ask him about the milk, Doc.

                    DOC
Why?

                    COACH
Why what?

                    DOC
I'm losing my mind.

                    COACH
Stay away from the water.

                    BILLY
It's not the water.

                    DOC
It isn't?

                    BILLY
No, it's the milk.

                    COACH
It is?

                    BILLY
No, it isn't.

                DOC & COACH
It isn't?

                    BILLY
It's the asbestos in the milk.

                    DOC
That's what that stuff is. I thought it was steel wool. We've got a big problem here.

                COACH & BILLY
Big big big!

THE DOC EXAMINES A LARGE VOLUME

                    DOC
Asbestos, let's see . . . Ergot, Dexedrine, Cocaine, Caffeine, Benzedrine, Acid, Aspirin, Amphetamines . . . ooops . . . Asbestos . . . Oh, oh!

Asbestos. This is a catastrastroke! The asbestos will sop up all the steroids we put in the milk!

COACH
I knew it! We'll never win the Alternate Olympics!

DOC
And the Mayor will lose his big bet!

BILLY
And Billville will become a second-class power!

DOC & COACH
Small small small!

*A CELESTIAL GONG PROCLAIMS THE ARRIVAL
OF REVOLUTIONARY CONSCIOUSNESS*

BILLY TRANSFORMS HIMSELF INTO A WORKER'S CADRE

BILLY
Suddenly, revolutionary consciousness strikes and the characters think differently.

MAYOR
I am Comrade PN, no longer pronounced Penisnose. I was Mayor of Billville, now spelled Bill Jing Ville. I am a reformed man. I am the village committee leader now. I sleep in my office for free. My wife was a prostitute. Now, she is a prostitute. It is my duty to strike and raise the consciousness of the Capitalist running dogs of Bill Jing Ville. The Doctor!

DOC
I am Doctor I. I was a member of the good old gang. I poisoned the wells. Those were the days. Now I labor incessantly to remove asbestos from the lungs of farmers and soldiers. I am a humble barefoot Doctor. (But no doctor ever died poor.)

MAYOR
The Doctor has healed himself. Now the Coach must run his race.

COACH
I am village teacher Dad. Once I injected steroids into students to cheat and exploit them. I made my children bigger to make myself feel bigger. Now I am completely reformed. Hell, you can bet on it!

DOC
What's the odds?

MAYOR
Yeah!

BILLY
I was exploited youth. They wanted to give me a big neck. I just wanted to neck in a big car. Now I desire to labor in the bicycle factory and raise gland-worms at night — in my big car.

ALL
We are the heroic statue that sits in the fountain of pure water at the corner of Bill Street and Bill in Bill Jing Ville. We are a living reminder to all who pass to post no bills and keep off the people's grass.

MAYOR
Ring ring. Oh, oh. Secretary's been relocated to the kapok tree plantation. I get it myself. It's the red phone. It's the President. Hello, Comrade. Where's all the Coca-Cola you promised? We've already sent the bicycles. Need any more painted eggs or pencil sharpeners? We've got a special on these little black shoes . . .

ALL
Everybody's wearing them!

THE CADRE, MAYOR, DOC AND COACH LIFT THEIR FEET TO DEMONSTRATE THEIR SOLIDARITY WITH LITTLE BLACK CHINESE SHOES

PROCLAIMING THE ULTIMATE VICTORY OF SOCIALIST SHOES OVER CAPITALIST RUNNING DOGS, THE WORKERS JOIN IN PATRIOTIC SONG!

EVERYTHING'S A SONG
(WE'RE THE 8 SHOES)
(THE 8 SHOES THEME SONG)

Music to the tune of "Happy Days Are Here Again"
Lyrics by Rothman & Klein

CHORUS:
How de do de, Hip Hooray!
We're the opening act, we hope you stay;
If you walk out on us, we get no pay!
We're the 8 Shoes — who are you?

VERSE:
I'm Mickey — Oly — Low Brow — Bud!
We've played every motel, bar and club;
Yes, the act is live, but the music's dubbed!
We're the 8 Shoes — who are you?

BRIDGE:
We love to sing and make music –
We hate when you sing along . . .
(Just kidding!)

CHORUS:
Come and see us when we're through,
We're in 503 and 502.
Yes, there's 4 of us for each of you!
Let the 8 Shoes Sock It To You!

[SIX BAR PATTER BREAK]

BRIDGE:
We love to drink and make whoopee!
Look out or we'll whoopee on you!
(Just kidding!)

CHORUS:
We've got jokes and dancin' feet.
When we're not on stage, we're in the street
So we hope you stay and warm your seat,
We're the 8 Shoes — we've got sole!

TAG: Everything's a song!

Lounge acts being what they are, material changes from club to club and maybe show to show, depending on the news. The Eight Shoes had a repertoire of songs for Presidential candidates. Let's start with a Blues . . .

THE EDMUND G. BROWN JR. BLUES

Jerry's got a heavy date
With his destiny.
Left the California Coast
USA to see.
When he went back East
They called him a flake
Carter wouldn't talk to him
And Teddy hit the brake!

CHORUS:
'Cause he's got zippers on his shoes,
Black hair that sings the blues,
A suit that don't make news,
And he knows he's going to lose.
Solar power makes him blind,
But Linda makes him mind!
He's got the Edmund, The Edmund G.
The Edmund G. Brown Jr. Blues.

The King of California
In hot water to his chin -
He stepped out to take a bath
And Mike Curb fell right in!
Jerry was a Jesuit,
Then he turned to Zen.
The sound of one hand clapping
Sounds like big applause to him.

CHORUS: 'Cause he's got . . .

The Gov would like to live in Space,
Far away from home.
Orbiting above his State
With Bucky in a Dome.
Anti-draft and – nuke –
Science-Fiction time!
He's twenty years ahead of us,
And twenty points behind!

CHORUS:
'Cause he's got zippers on his shoes,

Black hair that sings the blues,
A suit that don't make news,
And he knows he's going to lose.
Solar power makes him blind,
But Linda makes him mind!
He's got the Edmund, The Edmund G.
The Edmund G. Brown Jr. Blues.

What about Jimmy Carter? Peter and I had been arguing for quite a while about his Presidency, and the argument went on in our Eight Shoes tribute . . .

THE DEMOCRATIC SUCCESSION SONG

Well, we went down to Georgia
And we picked up a guy
And put him in a pickup
And we said "Why –
Not make him President?"

Jimmy Carter, he's our President!
Jimmy Carter, White House resident!
Are you from Hell?
Some say you're Heaven-sent!

Well, he's got a Brother name of Bill
Piled up beercans in a mile-high hill
An' you know what? Bill's got 'em still!

He's got a white-haired Mama name of Lil
Her foot in her mouth — she's fit to kill!
If the Lord don't help him
We know Lil will!

Jimmy Carter, he's our President!
Jimmy Carter, White House resident!
Are you from Hell?
Some say you're Heavensent!

He's got a faith-healin' Sister holds his hand
She's got that old-time religion
to beat the band!

(Let's see if she's got enough
to beat the Kennedys!)

He's got a Wife named Roselyn
She's a wonderful spouse
She's got a million-dollar staff
takes care of the House
(She does a pretty good job
on the Senate too!)

Now you met the ass-whumpin' Carters
Man they really slay me . . .

Wait a minute! You forgot one!
You mean sweet little Amy?

Because after eight years of Jimmy Carter
And after four years of Fritz Mondale
And after four more years
of that Fritz Mondale
And four years of Edmund G. Brown Jr.
And four years of Joseph P. Kennedy the 3rd
It'll be time for
Amy Carter
First Lady President
Amy Carter
The White House resident
She's cute as Hell!
Some say she's Heavensent!

By that prediction, Amy would have been the first woman President, elected in 2004. Instead (wisely, surely) after some time as an "activist," she retired from the political realm. In 1980, on the Republican side, the 8 Shoes still had it for Jerry Ford, the accidental, accident-prone former President . . .

THE REPUBLICAN FIGHT SONG

Yes, we need a Football President!
Yes, we need a man like Ford!
We need a man with a head that's shaped
Just like a great big pumpkin gourd!
Big! Big! Big!

We need a Golfer Prexy
Like Ike and Dick and Jane!
Yes, we need a Football President
If we're going to lose The Game!

Yes, we need a stupid President!
Yes, we need a "hunk" like Ford!
We need a man with a brain
That hasn't thought since 1944!
Four more!

Yes, we need a sleeping President
Because we need a man to blame!
Yes, we need a gourd like Ford aboard
If we're going to lose
If we're going to lose
If we're going to lose The Game!

The sketch that followed, "Meanwhile," subtitled "The Towel Play," mashed the Iran Hostages and the beleaguered Afghans together with randy Sailors out of a Forties MGM musical, and snow-bound Marin County Hottubbers. Each group wore their towels in particular ways — as blindfolds, turbans, post-bath wear and, well, not at all. In later versions, after the Hostages were released, their part of the piece was dropped. The fourth character who appeared in "In The Hot Tub Again" became one of the Fuddz, home after the band's breakup. (For reasons I may never get to, the role was later given to Hemlock Stones.)

For the album, we re-created the other three sketches in the studio and added an "off-stage" scene with the Fuddz. "The Four Gobs," "In The Hot Tub" and "In The War Zone" each became a stand-alone playlet.

MEANWHILE, or
The Invasion of Afghanistan
A Traditional Turkish Towel Play

1.
IN THE WAR ZONE

THE SCENE OPENS IN THE DESERT. THE WIND IS BLOWING. GOATS BLEAT. FOUR AFGHANS NAMED "AHMED," WEARING TOWELS FOR TURBANS, SING THE OPENING NUMBER TO THE TUNE OF "OKLAHOMA!"

PP: Aaaaaaaaa-fga-hanistan!
The sand is filling up my sox
And the goats and sheep can hardly sleep
With the Russians shooting from the rocks!

THREE SHOTS FROM THE DRUMMER

PB: Got my hashish!

DO: Got my gun!

PA: Got my stallion, we're Number One!

ALL: We've got our pipes in the morning
And our goats at night

PB: And with our pipe in the morning

PP: And our goat in the evening

ALL: We're all right!

BIG FINISH. THE WIND BLOWS. THE GOATS BLEAT. A HELICOPTER PASSES OVER, FIRING CANNON. THE WIND BLOWS.

AHMED 1: Hey, Ahmed!

AHMEDS: What?

AHMED 1: They didn't see us!

AHMED 2: Oooooooo!!

AHMEDS: What?

AHMED 2: They killed my goat! Those pigs!

AHMEDS: Ooooooo!!

AHMED 3: Quiet! Quiet! Here they come again!

AHMED 2: Get down! Get down!

AHMED 1: Shoot! Shoot!

AHMED 4: I will wipe them from the sky, brothers!

AHMED 3: Now! Now!

THE HELICOPTER PASSES BY AGAIN, FIRING.

AHMED 4: I'm trying! Ah! Camel snot!

AHMEDS: Ooooooooo!!

AHMED 4: There's sand in my British American-made French Israeli Belgian burp-gun again!

AHMED 3: Sons of the hills! Throw down that neo-Imperialist pro-colonialist, anti-Islamic devil stick! Use this Baryshnikov I arrested from the still white fingers of the little dead man beneath the tanks.

AHMED 4: Sodomized donkey meat! Pah! All those Baryshnikovs are defective!

AHMED 2: Maybe so, but they are so beautiful! And the bullets come with our names engraved on them!

AHMEDS: Ahhhhhh! Oooooooooh!

THE WIND BLOWS

AHMED 1: Ahmed!

AHMEDS:	What?
AHMED 1:	Is it not true that ever since we sacked the American Embassy we have picked up a lot of Westernist tendencies?
AHMEDS:	Ahhhhh! Oooooooh!
AHMED 2:	But how could we help it? They were lying around everywhere! In the color magazines! In the television! In the icebox!
AHMED 3:	What kind of beer was that?
AHMED 4:	Henry Winkler Private Reserve.
AHMEDS:	Ahhhhhhhhh!

AGAIN, THE HELICOPTER APPROACHES

AHMED 2:	Here they come again!
AHMED 3:	Sit on it!

THE HELICOPTER'S CANNONS FIRE

AHMED 2:	Ahhhhhhhhh . . .

THE 'COPTER FLIES AWAY

AHMED 1:	Ahmed . . . !
AHMEDS 3 & 4:	He's dead!
AHMED 1:	It was the will of God. See? The bullet had his name on it!

THE WIND CONTINUES TO BLOW

OH, AFGHANISTAN!
Or, "Bill" (Chanson Primitif)

When I come to Billville I had another name,
But the city ordinance makes us all the same!
Oh! Afghanistan!
Oh! Afghanistan!
I love Billville like a native son –
I change my name to Bill so I feel more like one!
Oh, Afghanistan!
Save us from Babylon!
If they can take your name away,
Can't they take us too?
They do!

I live in Billville on a street named Bill,
Near the corner of Bill Street and Bill!
Oh! Afghanistan!
Oh! Afghanistan!
I love Billville with a fierce pride!
I look for a girl named Bill to be Bill's bride!
Oh, Afghanistan!
Save us from Babylon!
If they can take your name away,
Can't they take us too?
They can, you know!

I work in the Bill Building with a Boss named Bill
Gonna have three kids, name 'em Bill, Bill, Bill!
Oh! Afghanistan!
Oh! Afghanistan!

We believe in a Big God named Bill,
The First and Last of the House of Bill!
Oh, Afghanistan!
Save us from Babylon!
If they can take your name away,
Can't they take us too?
They will!

People of Billville, we stretch out our hands!
Welcome all Bills to the Promised Land!
Oh! Afghanistan!
Oh! Afghanistan!

If in your heart you want to change your name to Fred
I and I pray to Big Bill to strike you dead!
Oh, Afghanistan!
Save us from Babylon!
If they can take your name away,
Can't they take us too?
If they can take your name away,
Can't they take us too?
Can't they take us too?
They do!

2.
THE FOUR GOBS ON THE SIDEWALK

FOUR SAILORS NAMED "HAPPY" ARE RELAXING IN THEIR HOTEL ROOM, EQUIPPED WITH A PIANO, ON WHICH "HAPPY PETE" IS NOODLING AND SINGING UNDER HIS BREATH. EACH GOB WEARS A POST-SHOWER TOWEL.

HAPPY PHIL: Holy Schlamoly!

HAPPY PETE: Huh?

HAPPY DAVE: Whaaaaa?

HAPPY PHIL: Say! Listen up, you gobs! I was just lookin' out the hotel window, and you know that great big news sign that goes around that funny lookin' building?

GOBS: Yeah . . .

HAPPY PHIL: Well, it just announced that the entire Fleet is being shipped out — in an hour!

GOBS: Oh, no!

HAPPY PHIL: So can the music, Happy.

HAPPY PETE: Okey dokes.

HAPPY PHIL: Let's get in our dress whites, gobs — 'cause I don't know about you guys, but, as for me . . .

GOBS: What?

HAPPY PHIL: Hit it, Happy!

HAPPY PETE: Got it! (HE PLAYS)

HAPPY PHIL'S SONG

I gotta get a gal!
A special kinda gal!
A gal who's got a house and a butler and a phone,
A special kinda girl with three kids she
calls her own!
Waiting for a call from me,
Because she's got an hour free!
I gotta get a gal, a super kinda gal,
A sooper-dooper gal, a super duplex kinda pal!
I gotta find a pearl, a very special kind of girl . . .
Who's married!

HAPPY PHIL (THE OTHER ONE): That sounds like the perfect kinda gal — and, gosh, I hope ya find her.

HAPPY PHIL: Thanks!

HAPPY PHIL: Just not in my house!

GOBS: Ha ha ha ha . . .

HAPPY PHIL: Aw, you know . . . But I always wanted a special kinda gal . . .

HAPPY DAVE: Well, what kinda special kinda gal is that, Happy?

HAPPY PHIL'S SONG (THE OTHER ONE)

I know the kind of gal I see . . .
A gal who doesn't talk to me . . .

PETE: Keep talkin', Happy!
A gal with staples cross her tummy!

DAVE:	What is he talkin' about? I know we'll always . . .
PETE:	Yeah? That she's a gal who'll always . . .
PHIL:	What? A little pal who'll always . . . (Now you'll get it!) Do it my way!
HAPPY DAVE:	Ah git the pitcher now, Happy! That's the kinda gal you kin fold right up and jest slip right inta yer front pocket, huh?
HAPPY PHIL:	That's what I have in mind. But what about you, Happy?
HAPPY DAVE:	Oh, er, what about me?

HAPPY DAVE'S SONG

Ah need a little lady
Who'll go the rounds with me!
A gal who'll really drink an'
Clown aroun' with me!
A gal who'll dance aroun',
An' paint the town,
An' fall right down — look out!
An' roll the other way
When we sleep it off — together!

GOBS (HARMONIZING): To-geth-er! Ya-hoo!

HAPPY PHIL:	Hey, Happy! You're just sittin' over there nude, noodlin' on the piano. What about you?
HAPPY PETE:	Aw, gee whiz, fellas . . .
HAPPY DAVE:	Aw, ya see? He's jest so shy he don' even hardly ever think about gals!

HAPPY PHIL (THE OTHER ONE): Hey, I always wondered what was inside that egghead of yours, Happy. What do you think about?

HAPPY PETE: You mean when I go back to the ship at night?

GOBS: Yeah . . .

HAPPY PETE: And lock the door?

GOBS: Yeah!

HAPPY PETE: And crawl into bed?

GOBS: Oh, yeah!

HAPPY PETE: What do I think about?

GOBS: Yeah!!

HAPPY PETE: I think about nuclear war!

GOBS: Nuclear war?

HAPPY PETE: Uh huh!

HAPPY PETE'S SONG

PETE: Gals are nothin' compared to Nuclear War!

DAVE: What did he say?

PETE: Gals are little and tear apart,
Not Nuclear War!

PHIL: I don't get it!

PETE: Gals are warm and gals have heart!
Blonds are dumb but bombs are smart!
If anything blows this gob apart
It won't be gals!

GOBS: What'll it be?

PETE: It'll be — Nuclear War!

GOBS (HARMONIZING): Waaaaaarrrrrrr!

3.
IN THE HOT TUB

THREE GUYS ARE IN A CALIFORNIA HOT TUB SOMEWHERE BETWEEN MONTECITO AND MARIN COUNTY. ONE OTHER GUY, "BALDY," IS UNDRESSING. FRENCH MUSIC — "LE TUB CHAUDE" — PLAYS IN THE BACKGROUND. THERE IS THE SOUND OF CUTTING COKE AND SNORTING. A GUY TAKES A HIT OF POT . . .

GUY: Oh, wow . . .

MAN 1: Look at the stars, man . . . wow! The stars . . . they're so . . . there's so many of 'em . . .

MAN 2: That's hot, man.

MAN 1: Really!

BALDY: For sure!

GUY: Whatever . . . oh, wow!

MAN 2: Oh, wow, yeah . . .

BALDY: Hey, guy? How's the divorce?

GUY: Oh, great. We divided our kids between our two lawyers.

MAN 1: Oh, wow! You got Solomon & Solomon, huh? Yeah, they divided our kid too.

MAN 2: That's hot.

MAN 1: Really!

BALDY: For sure!

GUY: Whatever! Oh, wow . . .

BALDY: OK. Watch out, guys. Hot stuff behind ya!

MAN 1: Oh, move over . . .

BALDY: Look at this, huh? I oughtta be in porno, huh? That's where the money is . . . Lemme have that . . .

MAN 1: Here. Here — smoke this . . .

BALDY: Oh, no . . .

MAN 1: I'll hold it for ya . . .

BALDY: Naw. Grass is for hippies . . .

MAN 2: Yes, ya know — me and the girlfriend, we really gotta move to a bigger house — but the bank wants the down in coke.

MAN 1: Money, man — it's tough. I had to pay my dentist bill with my gold fillings.

MAN 2: Go for it, man!

MAN 1: Really!

BALDY: For sure!

GUY: Whatever!

MAN 2: Oh, wow . . .

BALDY: Wow! . . .

GUY: Uh, hey!

MAN 2: What?

GUY: When I put the towel over my face like this, what do I look like?

BALDY: Gary Gilmor.

GUY: Nope. One of the hostages.

MAN 2: Ooooo! That's heavy!

MAN 1:	Yeah — who isn't?
BALDY:	For sure.
GUY:	Who isn't heavy, huh?
MAN 1:	No — who isn't a hostage.
GUY:	Oh, wow . . .
MAN 2:	Oh, wow . . .
BALDY:	For sure.
MAN 1:	Wow, man! Hey . . .
BALDY:	What?
MAN 2:	What?
MAN 1:	Is this — uh — hair? Hair in the hot tub? Gross, man!
GUY:	Gross-out!
BALDY:	Gross-OUT, man!
MAN 2:	No, man — that's — here — here, man — that's the Siamese seaweed soap, man.
MAN 1:	Oh . . .
BALDY:	Hey — long hair, short hair . . .
MAN 2:	What?
BALDY:	Hair is dead, huh?
MAN 2:	Yeah, right! Go for it, Baldy!
MAN 1:	Really!
BALDY:	Yeah, for sure!

GUY:	Whatever!
BALDY:	Oh, wow!
MAN 1:	Wow! Baldy . . .
GUY:	Hey, any of you guys think that maybe — uh — this hot tub is too hot?
MAN 1:	Oh, uh — ask Pam Jergonson, man. It's her hot tub. Gimme that joint . . .
MAN 2:	Uh, yeah — uh — where is Pam Jergonson?
GUY:	Pam, honey!
MAN 1:	She's around here somewhere . . .
BALDY:	Hey, look there — down there — in the Siamese seaweed.
ALL FOUR:	Oh, wow!
GUY:	Pam . . . poached . . .
MAN 2:	That's hot!
MAN 1:	Really!
BALDY:	For sure!
GUY:	Whatever!
ALL FOUR:	Oh, wow! . . .
MAN 1:	The stars, man . . .

THE NIGHT AND THE MUSIC FADE OUT TO THE SOUNDS OF CHOPPING AND SNORTING.

4.
IN THE ALLEY

BEHIND THE CLUB, JUST BEFORE THEY HAVE TO GO ON, THE FUDDZ ARE FIGHTING AMONG THEMSELVES . . .

GUITARMAN: . . . Back off! . . . Just rehearse it!

MANAGER: Will ya just rehearse it once?

KID: Will you just back off!

MANAGER: 'Ludes, 'ludes, 'ludes!

KID: I don' wanna rehearse, I wanna do it!

SMASHER: . . . in my beer!

MANAGER: What?

KID: There's asbestos in his beer!

MANAGER: Oh, come on!

SMASHER: . . . the group!

MANAGER: What?

SMASHER: What're you guys? Deaf? I think I'm gonna quit the group!

MANAGER: Aw, Smasher, you can't quit the group — your amp's in my van, man!

GUITARMAN: That's why it sounds like that!

MANAGER: Aw, leave him alone!

KID: Hey, you wanna go paint houses in the Valley with me? I'm ready to quit.

SMASHER: I thought I'd go an' work for my dad, OK?

GUITARMAN: I'll just rejoin the Dooby Brothers.

MANAGER: Hey, hey! Fuddz! Will you listen up, please? I just rented James Dean's car — the one he died in — and we put it in the — the drum set's in it and it looks so clean . . .

KID: Sick! Sicko! Sicko!!

MANAGER: So come on, let's get on stage!

KID: Are we hostages?

SMASHER: What does Jimmy Dean have to do with this?

MANAGER: What's wrong? What's the matter with this . . .

KID: Are we hostages?

MANAGER: What?

GUITARMAN: Sausages. With eyes!

KID: Sausages?

MANAGER: Wait a minute! That's good!

KID: Sausages with eyes!

MANAGER: Who are we? We are sausages!

EVERYBODY: We are sausages with eyes!
Who are we? We are sausages!
Sausages with eyes!

MANAGER: You realize that is a lyric, man?

SMASHER: Great lyric, man! Now we got two songs!

MANAGER: Hey! Hey, listen, man! We are Fuddz! Who else is gonna show them, huh, man?

EVERYBODY: We are Fuddz! Heh heh heh heh heh!!

WITH THE SMASH OF A BEER BOTTLE, THE FUDDZ COME ON . . .

VIOLENT JUVENILE FREEKS/ aka LOVE AGENT ORANGE
A Song by The Fuddz

Violent Juvenile Freeks!
Atom Mutant Geeks!
Babies born with asbestos pants
And fluorocarbon teeth!
Your parents fought in Nam and 'Gan
The desert's dead
They're back again,
Veterans of technocracy!
They love Agent Orange!
Love Agent Orange!

Junk food plastic wrap sack trash
Buried under your house for cash!
Kids grow up and their heads are mashed
With stupid air and TV hash!
Radiation everywhere!
But you don't care!
You're not alone!
You're on the phone!
(on hold!)

What's in that coke you're sniffing?
Sniff! What's in that Coke you're drinking?
Drinking . . . inking . . . inking . . .

Your Mother! Your Mother had to take three Valiums every day just to get up, huh? And she smoked three packs
of low-tar menthol cigarettes every day for nine months before you were born! She had to drink six cups of coffee just to stay awake! Yeah! And she had to take Quaaludes to sleep with
your Dad, and he works in the Insecticide Factory!
So how else can you expect to be anything but
mush-brained, Violent Juvenile Freekoids!
. . . oids . . . oids . . . oids

Hooked on mercury in your fish,
The brain-food ate your brain away!
Put some saccharine in your dish
With sodium nitrate bacon fry!
Nitrosamines are in your genes
And fill your pinhead pinball beer dreams
With Love Agent Orange!

245T-TCDD-DES-DD-TCE!
245TTCDDDESDDTCE!!

LOVE AGENT ORRRRANGGGE!!

5.
IN THE HOT TUB, AGAIN

THAT HOT TUB MUSIC IS PLAYING, BUT ONLY ONE MAN SITS IN THE TUB . . .

MAN: Aw, man . . . the stars . . .

AHMED, THE AFGHAN, STUMBLES IN, WHISTLING

AHMED: Where's my goat? Ah! You, in the hot tub! Where am I?

MAN: Uh . . . I . . .

AHMED: Is this Afghanistan?

MAN: Oh, no, man . . .

AHMED: Ah! Is it Iran?

MAN: No, man — it's Marin, man!

AHMED: Marin! Humm . . . Move over!

AHMED JOINS THE MAN IN THE TUB

MAN: I really like the way you wear your towel on your head, man.

THE KID ARGUES WITH SOMEONE, OFF, THEN ENTERS

KID: Get your hands off! I live here! Leave me alone! Hey, Dad! I quit the band again! Got any 'ludes?

MAN: Just paint the house, OK?

FROM THE SKY, VIA PARACHUTE, HAPPY PETE LANDS IN THE TUB.

HAPPY: Geronimooooooooo!!! OK! Everybody out of the hot tub! There's gonna be a Nuclear War!

MAN: Oh, did he say it was too hot in the hot tub, man?

AHMED: No . . . I think he said "everybody out of the icebox."

MAN: Oh, wow!

AHMED: Is this beer?

MAN: Oh, no — that's — that's seaweed shampoo, man.

KID: I don't believe this! Did you say nuclear war?

HAPPY: You got it!

KID: We'll be boiled like sausages — with eyes!

HAPPY: Hey, look! There's no time left! We're gonna have to do it the Navy way! Wrap the towels around your heads so you won't be blinded by the blast!

MAN:	Oh, that's hot. I'm gonna be nuked to death and all I've got on is Pam Jergonson's extra towel!
HAPPY:	Hey, don't you dip-sticks get it? They're gonna take us in a ball! I mean — this is Ground Zero, heroes! Hey! Don't any of you dudes want to escape?
MAN:	Escape? Oh, man! If this isn't escape, what is?
AHMED:	Really!
MAN:	For sure.
KID:	Whatever!
EVERYBODY:	Oh, wow . . .

By the end of the first week of March, after a successful run, it seemed to me we were on the edge of something new. Somehow it looked like MGM was interested our "Odyssey" idea, whatever it was. The "Fighting Clowns" album was set for production the next week. *Everything is moving very rapidly.* I was driving to and from LA almost daily.

Sat March 15 — LA
Drove into LA for studio day Wed — stayed Wed nite & drove back Thurs nite. Drove back Fri am and stayed last night. Wed we listened to all the music takes and made our choices. PB was totally stopped on the project & it made a very frustrating couple of days until we broke thru at the end of the session Fri — I had worked out an org. scheme which worked & just had to get everyone to buy it — just to have somewhere to start. Worked on a couple more songs Thu — very pleasant in the studio — they love us, good service, drugs everywhere. Fri we got into it — sweetening Bozos Song — just sounded great & got everybody high on the project.

Of course, in Hollywood, never did true love run smooth, nor movie business deals. "The Odyssey," no more than an idea on the Ides of March, mutated into a monster right from the beginning. There were these guys, see? Remember them? I'll call them H&G and somehow they got to be repping us at Metro.

We met Mr. H at a Mexican restaurant nearby the studio, not really a studio anymore, since its historic trappings were sold down to the carpet tacks a decade before along with the equally historic backlot, now condos, of course. *Everyone looked pretty spiffy.* I certainly did — I was wearing Howard Keel's Western shirt from "Annie Get Your Gun." I'd got it at the MGM auction.

As usual, the four Firesigns had arrived at different times from different places and never had that little conference before lunch which might have saved us a lot of trouble. Mr. H took great offence at something Peter said and *went off his rocker, said he was off the picture and left.* Whoo boy!

Fortunately, we called our new agent *who as fortune & good business methods wld have it, was waiting at the Thalberg bldg. for us. Pleasant man named Steve Gerrard — went to the meeting w/us.* The meeting turned out to be with the head of production, Richard Shepherd, a producer known best for "Breakfast at Tiffany's."

The meeting was super-pleasant — they really seem to want US to write and star in a movie — didn't care a rat's ass about H&G — & we came out of there in a pouring rain to have Oona take our photos — 4 happy guys with their MGM contract.

Back to Hollywood in the pouring rain to meet with another manager, a veteran in the rock business, John Hartmann. *I was impressed with him.*

As March melted into April we finished the "Fighting Clowns" album, with its awesome Jeff "Skunk" Baxter guitar overdubs and, at really the last minute, the elusive linkages between the pieces and Phil Austin's closing song, written by the two of us in the studio as the mix-down continued.

THIS BUS WON'T GO TO WAR!

There were 10 little Bozos sittin' on a Bus
One joined the Navy, now there's 9 of us
9 little Bozos sittin' in the Draft
One went crazy and the rest all laffed
8 dumb Bozos ridin' in a Van
If they can't get there then no one can

CHORUS: Everyone's a Bozo on this Bus
Zips and Beaners sittin' next to us
Are you a hostage? Are you a spy?
Or just some Berserker who's prepared to die?

We left 8 stupid Bozos sittin' in a tub
One got poached and had to leave the club
7 mellow Bozos with their brains all fried
One threw in the towel and the rest all cried
6 frightened Bozos tied up in a spot
One dove out the window but the rest got caught

CHORUS: Everyone's a Bozo on this Bus
Zips and Beaners sittin' next to us
Are you a hostage? Are you a spy?
Or just some Berserker who's prepared to die?

5 red-nosed Bozos burnin' in the sand
Things got so hot that one joined a band
That left 4 and there ain't no more
The driver got in and closed the door
4 angry Bozos with no place to hide
The bus pulls out and we're on the ride!

HOT GUITAR BREAK

There was never any doubt that the 4 would make it
They kicked out the driver and they said "Let's take it!"
They can afford to be Bozos on a Bus
'Cause they ain't afraid to use the word "us"
One thing's sure for the final 4
They know this Bus won't go to war!

CHORUS: Everyone's a Bozo on this Bus
Zips and Beaners sittin' next to us
Are you a hostage? Are you a spy?
Or just some Berserker who's prepared to die?

Finally worked thru all the various ideas & came out w/something very simple & introductory which reminded us all of Bozos — this album seems almost a segue from the end of Bozos — seemed to work & was in fact the only agreement we cld reach — main worries being self-consciousness & too much (or too little) plot.

As the fortunes of the record business would have it, "Fighting Clowns" was finally released by our friends at Rhino. I've always loved Fred Jones' vivid production and mix with its combination of live and studio, its immediacy, even the tensions running at the surface. I can only imagine what might have been produced if we'd included "Billville" or more of the 8 Shoes in a two-record set.

With three almost completely different stage shows, comprising our usual ripe TV comedy, two different Nick Danger plots, the self-contained almost-album "Joey's House," and up-to-the-minute political satire, augmented by the on-going writing for NPR, you would think we'd be able to lift a simple dumb movie script out of the pages already written. No, no, we had to tackle "The Odyssey!"

CHAPTER 7
THE ODYSSEY

1.

The voyages of Ulysses were to be undertaken from an office on a shady San Fernando Valley side street bordering one of moviedom's oldest studio lots, with a nice little bridge spanning the concrete channel of the Los Angeles River. I suspected that the row of offices had been the writer's bungalows for long-gone Republic Pictures, makers of B-movies and Roy Rogers' Westerns. That seemed appropriate.

Unfortunately, there was no money in our contract for housing. Since I had to spend most of the next couple of months at work on the movie, I made the uncomfortable choice of sleeping on the office couch. Since Tinika, who had visited briefly, was off back to Norfolk VA and planned to travel to Europe in May, we had a house-sitter in Santa Barbara. How could I have been in two places at once? Trust me, it was Nowhere At All!

It didn't take long for us to get started. In a couple of days we had posters on the walls and a bulletin board stuck with notes and we had aired our various concepts: *PA really starts from a pretty faithful interpretation of The Odyssey. PP was beginning from a complete "comedy-izing" of it that began to place more emphasis on the back-story (a "Russians Are Coming" idea — sailors on the Poseidon sub etc). I really brought or emphasized the gods — the fantasy aspect — "plot doesn't matter." My suggestion that PA play our Ulysses was immediately accepted by PP & silently by PB (PA worried abt Peter having a part "important" enough to satisfy him).*

We hadn't got much further than that when the H&G team showed up. Mr. G arrived on our doorstep *to bring us small bits of news.* Behind him was Mr. H, *on crutches, his face ashen pale, in pain, his foot bandaged and swollen. He came in, sat down.* Then came some swell movie dialog:

AUSTIN: What are you here for? What do you want?

MR. H: I've decided to come back, accept MGM's offer to produce the picture.

BERGMAN: That's not our agreement.

MR. H: I have to live up to my responsibilities.

BERGMAN (TO MR. G): I don't have a lot of confidence in you, if you can't control yr partner.

AUSTIN: You said you were out!

And with that, Phil handed back Mr. H the $20 bill that he'd tossed on the table when he'd stalked out of the restaurant. It had been stuck on our bulletin board as a weird trophy. *Lots more went down — all very Mickey Mouse as PB pointed out. Finally it seemed to be a stalemate — Mr. H was stuck in a chair & if he did have something to say, wouldn't say it.*

His partner, Mr. G sat silently, Peter fumed. That was it! I got up, *stood in front of the pathetic Mr. H and said (first) I didn't want to spend my time w/him being a psychiatrist (then, as it occurred to me) that this was MY office & (tho I'd put my shoes on) I wasn't going to leave it — he was. I went over & opened the door & told him to use it. In a great display of humiliation he limped out, clutching the $20. It was a dog-skirmish — I won — at least this bout.*

Mr. G explained that he'd brought Mr. H along on purpose, so that all four of us would tell him he was "out." We were never going to see Mr. H again! It was hard to get Mr. G out of the office — *he's a door-lingerer — they all want to be with us — brrrr!!*

We broke at 4 pm, after casting yrs truly as Poseidon and Proctor as Hermes the Trickster. Peter would become a hipster sidekick of Austin's — our Ulysses whom we'd call "Bill."

The writing continued for the cruelest month of April. *We go at it hard — PP often w/irate peevishness or impatience. PA patient & thoughtful. PB close to the book, brings it in whenever an idea is needed.* As hard as we went at it, by the end of the month we'd run fresh out of fresh ideas and the deadline for our 30-page story treatment was close. We had to finish.

I live in this office. Electric clock. I have a bottle of wine & listen to the TV on the radio. Pinup pix on the wall & a bumpersticker that says "Beaver Power." A Papoon For President T-shirt. Two dead decanters of Jim Beam. Outside this world, there's hardly a world. For now, I just live in this office.

2.

As luck would have it, Peter and I were invited to teach at the brand-new Midwest Radio Theatre Workshop in early May. We flew into Columbia MO (where the Workshop would be held for the next fifteen years), arriving just before the last eatery closed. It offered 3.2 beer and stale pizza and we accepted. In our seminar the following day *we emphasized simplicity & improvisation & were "light" in contrast to Yuri R's acting and exercise workshops.* That would be Yuri Rasovsky, a radio drama producer celebrated as "El Fiendo," a long-time colleague and friend. Another colleague, Charles Potter, was also teaching that first year.

Guest celeb from the world of "Old Radio" was Jim Jordan, a star with his wife Marion of the long-running comedy "Fibber McGee and Molly." I'd listened to many episodes of the show and was a fan of its perfect combination of writing, acting, sound effects and production, so it was great to hang out with the somewhat fragile gentleman on a tour of a local historic mansion where we sat together on what they claimed was Harry Truman's old couch. That's about as unforgettable as you can get!

Pete and I returned to the Studio City office suffering from bad moods. I was beginning to resent the *severe dislocation of my life required by this work schedule.*

Suddenly, Austin arrived in a funk. He had fundamental problems with the 13 page story outline we'd labored on so far. He was angry and frustrated about it and I felt that his suggestions ran *counter to his on major contributions to the outline.*

Scylla, meet Charybdis! I'm sailing right between ya! Circe's warning to Ulysses: "Hug Scylla's crag, sail on past her, top speed." Well, Scylla may have looked like a rock, but it was really a six-headed stop-motion monster that picked us off one by one.

I was the solitary inhabitant of my island office, marooned in Studio City. *Well — I don't know — too too emotional — it's clearly a mad time.*

At home in Santa Barbara, I had been burgled. TV, stereo, the usual. I found about that at the beginning of *two days that shook my world.* There were continuous interruptions as the four of us *were in the midst of trying to clarify what PA meant by his depths of emotion when approaching the subject.* Phil questioned each aspect of the story outline, we talked it all out again, beat by beat, and *I left still thinking there was something left of the original — I ended today explaining my view of* THIS *version as "another movie."*

Austin countered, *"We can do Art on NPR — this is a movie — we're here to pick up those big checks!"*

Back in S. B. I surveyed the damage, changed the locks and had a whirlpool of conversations spinning in my brain. Lash me to the mast, boys! Austin, so far as I could tell, had decided to approach this job as purely a professional assignment and *as something that, at all costs, stands a chance of getting made because it's a balls-out comedy w/no intellectual pretentions.* OK, so this wouldn't be a unique Firesign product. It would be *another H'wood comedy w/"funny dialog" (as PA kept saying) & gag scenes. Raise no objections, go with the flow* I told myself and that served me well during the next writing day, which included reducing our original takes on most of the immortal scenes from "The Odyssey" to six in the final "new" treatment.

I was getting sicker in my sweaty bed couch. Heading toward bronchitis. My marriage to Tinika was washing up on on a distant, rocky shore. I'd told her, if she'd decide to come back home, I'd be willing to give up half my Firesign time to be with her. She was afraid of "losing herself" and jealous of us, afraid of always being an adjunct to Firesign, a "girl with the band." She was traveling and put off giving me an answer.

Sick and depressed as I was, I still spent another couple of nights on the couch. The next day began with Peter, who had a "new idea" and sat down and wrote it. *It turned out to be the scene in Troy where the boys try to sell chickens to Turks.* That one didn't make it all the way to the First Draft, but it indicates the craziness we began with. Actually, the First Draft screenplay opens like this:

FADE IN:

EXT. OPEN OCEAN — DAY

A ten-foot high plastic chicken floats in the midst of the Atlantic. Printed on its side, in English and Turkish, is "Eat Me." Two men, BILL ODYSSEUS and CRAZY GEORGE, are riding on top. It is hard to hold on to the slippery chicken.

"The boys," Bill and Crazy George, are being watched from Mt. Olympus by the gods, most of whom are suffering from hangovers. It's a sort of Heavenly Hills mansion with a nice, classical swimming pool.

ANOTHER ANGLE

A large, white BULL sleeps and snores loudly. He has gilt horns with a laurel wreath draped over one of them. HERA, a large, pleasant woman, stands over him. She is the only thing stirring. She pokes the bull in the ribs.

> HERA
> Dear . . . Zeus, dear.
> You've got to get up.

The bull snores loudly.

> HERA
> (continuing)
> Zeus! Really, dear.
> That thunderous noise . . . it's embarrassing.

For the first week or so of our remaining month on the job, I wasn't able to return to the big city. I went home from the office on May 20, my bronchitis confirmed. The day before, Austin and I finally had a long walk along the L.A. River-bank and *good and friendly talk. PA seemed to reveal his problem — I was surprised to see it was the same as mine — the office — 40 hr week — boredom — exhaustion w/talk talk talk & constant debate.*

3.

We had begun to write separately or in pairs even before I went home and that's the way it went while I settled in to get well. It was chilly and foggy in Santa Barbara. I wondered, *could it be the volcano? Most interesting news in ages, if a touch cataclysmic.* Mt. St. Helens, of course. My wonderful Mom took care of me as did faithful, fat Humboldt the cat.

Our new manager, John Hartmann, (he'd been EVERYBODY's manager!) was friends with Julia Phillips, the Oscar-winning producer of "The Sting," "Taxi Driver" and "Close Encounters." Julia had a dinner which I was too sick to attend and I heard about it from Austin.

Apparently it was weird, with P&B "on," Famous Amos there too — Oscar on her desk. "Everything has its price" Phil kept saying. She loves Hartmann, loves FT, has LBMayer's office & 7-picture deal & wants "us" to work on a script for her. Thought PA was "the serious one." No women allowed at the dinner. Phil glad I wasn't there in a weakened condition — wondered what would have happened had I been there w/bells on.

I felt so good that it was even good to talk to PA & hear all this stuff. The muck gets deeper & stickier all the time — it's H'wood more than anything else — so much money riding on — on movies — which are now something very un-nostalgic. I fear that jungle — it attracts and repels — I can't play its game. How interesting to be sought-after w/out making any moves for it.

Hollywood Reporter, July 10, 1980

"Close Encounters" had been released three years before and Hollywood is a "what have ya done lately, what are you on now?" kind of place. While the four of us wrote, re-wrote and re-re-re-wrote, high-heels were afoot in Tinseltown. By the end of May we had finished a brand-new 36-page prose treatment. Editing that down to about half and getting rid of all our clever stuff related to the original Homer and with Bill's solo turn as a CW star, we started and re-re-re-started. We had two more weeks as screenwriters to get the thing finished. If this ain't Hollywood by the book, Peter Lorre was the Fat Man!

I find the writing easy, actually — the vision of the scene is pretty clear — I work fairly fast & editing is easy as always. I'm not married to any of it — just want to keep it fast moving & funny, I've decided, & write good dialog for POSEIDON just in case we make this turkey.

Back in the office, I felt Peter was down. Things weren't going well in his home life, among the other problems we all had, which included, the money was running out, and *he was "going crazy" from only writing — from being a "professional writer." PA also admitted to being "stir-crazy." Actually, I feel fine — I like to see the pages pile up — the writing I do goes smoothly & easily — the first draft is looking better and better.*

If only. The dreaded H&G called in to report that one of the producers, Willi Hunt, hated the Story Outline and we were all supposed to have a meeting the next afternoon. Oh, geeze! *I decided I didn't need to go through that — & couldn't.* Let H&G and our OTHER manager Steve just *go and take notes, or cldn't we wait until this 1st draft was done?*

Austin announced he'd go, since he didn't trust H&G to get anything straight. Peter said, "OK, I'm calling Willi Hunt," *which I said took guts & which PA sd "no — just a star calling the studio."* Honestly, the fantasy world they live in! It turned out, of course, that H&G had created a nice black hole in our day, Willi *just had a few questions* and there was nothing to worry about. There wasn't, of course, Peter just needed some back-scratching and had gone about it in the wrong way.

We continued to cut, punch up and hand final pages over to our typist, Bob. (No computer programs for that film-script-style in those days!) What "The Firesign Theatre's Odyssey" finally came down to, besides the opening at sea and the sequences on Mt. Olympus, was six basic sequences based on a combination of Homer and each of us in character, writing for ourselves.

Nausicaa, Calypso and the Sirens come first, at Sweet Beaver College where our heroes wash up on the beach. Cyclops and the cannibal Laestrygonians meet up with Bill and Crazy George at Road Hog Island where the burgers are reeel fresh. Circe turns men into cops ("pigs") at the Windy City Bozo Fair. The sun god Helios has a Ranch out in the Arizona desert where the Gods vacation. Our boys get stoned on ambrosia there and swallowed down the drain of the Sun God's pool. Finally, in Ithica, California, Bill arrives just in time to savage the suitors and win back his wife, Penny.

I retained my role as Poseidon throughout the two months of writing. As I re-read the script today I wonder how I might have carried off the part of the god and his four disguises — a distinguished lecturer, a balls-out leather biker, a Texas sheriff and the Governor of California. After all, only a couple of weeks before, "The Shining" had hit the nation's screens and Jack Nicholson's mad face was everywhere. Jack and I were both 43 in 1980. There was no comparison.

Speaking of the competition, the biggest movie of the year, "The Empire Strikes Back," starred ruggedly handsome Harrison Ford, six years my junior. The other movie comedies of the year would include "Airplane!" with its recycled star names; "Caddyshack," releasing a new low tide of Chevy Chase flicks, and Mel Brooks' "History of the World, Part One," with one of his terrific ensemble casts. On the femme side, "9 to 5" and "Private Benjamin" introduced enduring stars, including Lily Tomlin, who had reportedly walked out on one of our Roxy shows. Our modest, non-intellectual, now, hopefully, stupid comedy would have been up against, say, Robin Williams' debut in "Popeye." The stars of our generation were out and glittering. Somebody else was writing their scripts.

4.

When we were first (and last) in the film business, writing the rock-Western "Zachariah" in the old Thalberg Building as the MGM-that-was vanished into sleezybucks, I was only in my early 30s. 1970 was a fine year for smart comedies. Gene Wilder (three years older than I) and Donald Sutherland (a year older) starred in a great spoof of swordplay movies, "Start the Revolution Without Me." Sutherland also starred in "M*A*S*H" the same year, with Eliot Gould (a year younger). Mike Nichols' black comedy "Catch-22" starred Alan Arkin (2 years older). I love all these actors, but if I'd been destined to be a film star, I'd have gone to work at 18 when I auditioned with my Pomona College classmate Richard Chamberlain at (yep) MGM back in 1956. Dick became Dr. Kildare. I ended up in The Firesign Theatre. No regrets.

The first draft of "The Firesign Theatre's Odyssey" was off the press by mid-June. I got a copy at home in Santa Barbara, read it and enjoyed it. Thank the Gods!

Chapter 7: The Odyssey

EXT. THE BALCONY OVERLOOKING EARTH — DAY

Zeus, Hermes, and Poseidon look down over the railing at the Earth below.

> ZEUS
> Ye gods, we must have been asleep
> for two thousand years! Look at those
> big bright spots. All the little towns seem
> to have run together. It's so smoky! I need
> my telescope.

> POEIDON
> WHERE ARE MY WHALES? Look! There
> used to be a lot more whales than THAT,
> didn't there?

> ZEUS
> (peering through the scope)
> There's nothing but MORTALS! They're
> everywhere! Look at that! They didn't used
> to be over there. Or there. Or there. I hate
> mortals! Except the young female ones.

>   POSEIDON
> They come — they go. They're
> here today, and —
> (looking down)
> STILL here today!
>
>   ZEUS
> Dumb little guys. Short, short lives.
> Do they live longer than crickets or
> is it the other way around? I forget.

Who knows? Maybe Zeus would have been played by Robin Williams or Chevy Chase? John Goodman was nowhere to be seen in 1980. Maybe in the second draft the dialogue might be sharper? I forget.

The Julia Phillips affair continued. A dinner was planned, no wives were invited, but since Tinika had just arrived from Europe, I asked if she could come along. Julia would be delighted. That dinner was called off. Hartmann thought she was perhaps thinking through his pitch to her. *He ran down her apparent interest in TFT — "all phases — TV, B'way, movies." Her gossip was that The Odyssey was "in trouble" at MGM. Her apparent feeling was that we needed an "introduction" — in HER movie which she is persisting in trying to get us to "help" with. Something to do w/her "I Love The Movies" seems a quid pro quo for a "3 picture deal" w/her. "The Odyssey" remains at MGM w/possible Begelman mtg next week.*

Wait a minute! Stop right there! Suddenly the studio executive was the notorious David Begelman! This was the guy who had founded one of the big talent agencies, CMA. He ascended to the throne at Columbia Pictures in 1973 but he turned out to be a serial check-forger, caught by actor Cliff Robertson and quietly fired from Columbia in 1978. Now he was CEO and President of MGM! Only in Hollywood!

Alas, our audition was not with Begelman, but some cigar-smoking hard-looking flack named Chassman, who brought his flacks along to get together with our flacks. None of their flacks knew the Firesign Theatre (Marx Bros. maybe) and they were ready for a performance. We had been told *we wldn't be called upon to perform, exactly, but we'd be expected to flesh out verbally the scenes. I still thought it was to be a mtg with writers — wrong!*

Firesign and the flacks — *it was awkward — he really expecting some sort of performance, but not a "script reading," a "Make Me Laff" situation. We all did some good & fancy talking. PA began, then hung out. I had a lot to say & did the only comedy bit — "interview" w/a beer-bottle mike to one of the ladies present —*

but it dragged & was not su-pah until somebody — PB? — mentioned our movies — I want to see it, sd Chassman.

Astonishingly, neither the 1975 film version of our album, "Everything You Know Is Wong" nor our 1972 live stage performance, "The Martian Space Party" had been brought to these folks' attention. There we were, in them, on screen, performing. Well, *they'd have to see it now — & it IS what we do.*

A few days later we heard "Willi sez it's a go-ahead for sure when Begelman comes back." Hartmann told us *that it's pretty sure to go to 2nd draft & "assignment to a director." But it's not FerShur & must wait til after Aug 5.*

Summer ambled on in Fiesta City. My daughter Alizon, just 21, announced she was going to get married. Tinika had returned and we were on good terms. Firesign now had a regular Wednesday meeting with our Management in their offices at Crossroads of the World, a sort of office-village on Sunset Blvd. featuring a central art-deco ocean-liner building with portholes and a large globe suspended high above on a spindly tower. I loved the place, which was built back in my year, 1936, and where my father had an office in the early 1940s.

15 August — Well, another week ends & this waiting stretches out into the past & future — like Odysseus moping on Circe's shores.

PB still terribly restless & frustrated at lack of performance mode.

PP seeming to restrict his interest in FT to the "visual media" — expressed himself as being unsure he could continue unless FT achieved the big success. First time I'd heard him say anything like that.

If Julia Phillips had interest in us for a TV project, we were enthusiastic about offering her a series using some of our old Magic Mushroom radio ideas, each a broad genre spoof, starting with the original staged version of "The Giant Rat of Sumatra," already quickly adaptable to television.

I was still upset abt lack of forward motion & had 3 talks — one w/the group in which PB's and my anxiety level abt not working showed too much & bothered PA — another w/PA to smooth out his nervousness abt my nervousness — he actually very calmed in the face of this delay — said after MGM mtg & his depression then ("mostly at not getting out of town on time" he sd) decided not to worry abt it. Did want to do Roxy & also mentioned getting to work on a new album (!) w/Fred — "one a year."

I know, it was a big jump from my claustrophobia of early May to a need to keep working, and in the Summertime at that. It was a case of Peter's influence on me to take sides with him against Phil Austin. This happened more than once during our years and never turned out well. I think this time it was all about our perpetual shortness of immediate cash and fear of losing the income, more than the movie, which we knew could be lost, stolen or given to a couple of other writers any time now.

At home, *patio garden looking good — beans & zuchs, green tomatoes.* In the midst of solving the geometrical problem posed in making a curving brick path I got a call from Hartmann — *news is that we are on hold behind the Zuckers — Airplane! is so hot a hit this summer that they seem to be writing their ticket all over town.*

We were on hold. It was time to leave town.

Chapter 7: The Odyssey

I saw my son Devin off to the San Francisco Conservatory of Music for his first year and Alizon married to Anthony Harris (whose father produced "The Blob"!) that 1980 Summer. Tinika and I spent some time on Peter's woodsy property in Mendocino County. *He is talking hard abt moving from BHills to a combination of Mendo and Silver Lake to save the rent. Wants a total devotion to FT & will "make himself available." I gather [he's] essentially thru w/the P&B experience.*

Shortly after we left Mendocino, Tinika got a call offering her a job with the Santa Fe Arts Festival and left for New Mexico a couple of days later. I occupied myself trying to make order out of the pile of performance scripts we'd accumulated, in case we were going to develop a new show that also included old material.

Music in SB was great — a Grisman/Grapelli show, Count Basie, Bonnie Raitt and Muddy Waters, Charles Lloyd. My college chum Dick Chamberlain (we were in "The Crucible" together) was starring in Shōgun on NBC — five episodes stretched over the week — a brand-new idea in TVland and we were glued in rapt groups to the set.

It was a hot Summer in LA and by the end of September I'd been back and forth for meetings, one with Chris Bearde, writer on "Laugh-In" and creator of the "Sonny & Cher Comedy Hour" and "The Gong Show." A very pleasant Brit, he mainly wanted to pitch us on developing a *"fucking good idea" for a 5-nite 3—min strip show. I finally interjected the idea of a Theatre as "format" which seemed to go down just fine with everybody. Mtg over — we are now supposed to come up w/10 pp of this format.*

I took a few days "off" to visit Santa Fe in Festival Season, then came back for an important meeting at AVCO-Embassy with Kim Jorgensen, who'd produced "Kentucky Fried Movie" a couple of years before. Austin had arranged this, outside of Firesign. We'd always written pretty smoothly together and the Firesign foursome hadn't been fully on the same page for months. The meeting *was abt an "Airport" style satire of 50s SF movies. The guy we were supposed to take the mtg w/wasn't there — what a comedy! Did have mtg w/story people & it was pleasant enuf. PA sd how he liked those sorts of mtgs — where ideas are just ad libbed abt. How I hate 'em! Donno if anything will come out of it as usual.*

How cynical of me to have written that. I actually do like to sit around and ad lib ideas, so long as somebody is writing them down! Money helps too. However . . . *things going forward on TV project — that is, Bearde gets to take a mtg next week. But I like him and trust him to do his best.*

We heard that MGM, whoever they were at the moment, didn't like "The Odyssey." Things were moving ahead at AVCO, however, and we decided to prepare a new

"Evening With" show for the Roxy and The Road, opening in San Francisco. Peter would have liked to do "Fighting Clowns" again, but finally as rehearsals and rewriting continued much of the music was eliminated and we did some up-dating for the 8 Shoes show since Reagan had been elected on the 4th of November.

PA seemed very together — self-conscious abt being 40 — "surviving" — reconciling his gut-urge to be a loner w/the reality of collab & comp. I feel sorrier for him than for me. I am going to focus strongly on getting my own act going in the next 2 years.

PP spends all his time cleaning. He makes very few contributions — as usual, its PA and me doing the "writing."

We kept having meetings, thanks to John Hartmann. One with Zoëtrope's development director, Susan Rogers, to whom we proposed "The Giant Rat of Sumatra." What might that have become? Peter Cook and Dudley Moore had done a sendup of "The Hound of the Baskervilles" a couple of years before. It might have made a good model and our silly premise of the missing Zeppelin Tube and Chicago gangsters in the 1920s gave it an American Goon Show twist anyway.

PA & I seem in like Flynn on "Saucer!" — we had a "creative mtg" on that — but no money is forthcoming there either.

1980 was wrapping up. I celebrated my birthday with the last of a decade-long series of theme parties I shared with my birthday brother, Bob Blackmar. We supplied the guests with Polaroid cameras and set them to taking pictures. The theme was the movies and our joint invitation featured the two of us as director and cameraman.

Southern California twilight is a Technicolor kind of *noir*. Life had a very twilight feel that winter, even in Santa Barbara. As if none of us would ever do this again. As if none of us would ever be the same. It was The Eighties.

It was a very different "tour" we were facing this time. So far we were going to open (and close) on Thursday, December 11, two shows at a nightclub, the Old Waldorf in San Francisco's huge waterfront financial district. Just to give you the context, Rick Derringer was rockin' on Tuesday and Wednesday and Tower of Power would be boogiein' on Friday and Saturday. Food, beer, champagne (Chateau Natalie was only a Hamilton a bottle, Mumms Cordon Rouge set you back a Grant), and that same 10 bucks would buy all the well drinks you'd be able to keep down for an evening of comedy on the town.

December 10th John Lennon was killed on a Manhattan street. The LA Times headlines were big and black the next morning. That was how I heard about it. It was tragic, horribly stupid and very unsettling. Really, anybody could be out there with a gun. No one was armed and violent at the Old Waldorf, but it was spelling the end of our performing in clubs that served alcohol, and they all did.

Next show, just before Christmas in San Diego, was in a *club w/low ceilings & 4 lites out front — "no guns" warning at the door. Creepy, but an enthusiastic aud & two pretty good shows. Another two shows at the Roxy — all went well, w/the show coming together — 8 Shoes strong & ND coming into focus. 2nd show off the peak & distracted by a drunk heckler — fuck clubs!*

Don't know where it's going. The future is completely cloudy. Big questions abt FT's future must be asked/& answered w/in the next mo or so — & P & I must write a movie by then as well.

And so 1980 ended at last with *the repetitious rhythms of the Ayatolla and the endless ring of Lennon's "Starting Over."*

Cameraman Blackmar with Director Ossman

CHAPTER 8
A NEW AMERICAN PAGEANT

We were still billing the show as "Fighting Clowns," and the Acts (in order of randomness) were 1. 8 Shoes present America's Pageant; 2. Fighting Clowns/Towel Play; and 3. Nick Danger and Co. — "Frame Me Pretty."

This is a post-election version of "The American Pageant," endlessly revised from the original one that appears on our second album, different even from the variations we had done during the Leap Year Roxy run. Following Reagan's election in November, this one includes Peter's solo song, "Gotta Jump Down" and his homecoming scene in character as the incoming President.

It was done pretty much at top speed and was an exhilarating performance piece, with a Sound Poem performance using political names to imitate a steam train slowly starting off, running smooth, hitting rough tracks and arriving with a burst of steam — Bussssshhhhh.

THE 8 SHOES PRESENT "THE AMERICAN PAGEANT"

HEY, REAGAN!

Hey, Reagan! Reagan! Reagan!
You're not too old — old — old!
And it's never too late
To lose again!
Hey. Reagan! Reagan! Regan!
You're not too gray — gray — gray!
And it's never too late
To fade away!
Hey, Reagan! Reagan! Reagan!
He-e-ey, Reagan!
Wa-hoo! Wa-hoo!

Hey, Ronnie baby!
I mean we really love ya, Ronnie! We love ya!
We love the beautiful wrinkles on your face, Ronnie, baby!
I mean — it's a great old face we used to watch on the Late Late Show on TV. We can't see ya anymore, Ronnie, because you're runnin' — yes, you're runnin' and you're runnin' hard!
But the thing I like best about ya, Ronnie, is that hair of yours! That Superman-colored hair! Baby! Ronnie!
It gives me faith in ya, Ronnie! I love ya!
I love ya, Ronnie, baby!

'Cause we believe in ya! We believe in ya! We believe in ya!
We believe in ya, Ronnie! And we wantcha to listen to the Eight Shoes' advice, Ronnie! Lemme tell ya one thing, honey!
And this is what it is — keep it up! Keep it up! Keep it up!
(Git down!) Keep it up!

Keep it up, Reagan! Reagan! Reagan!
You're not too old — old — old!
And it's never too late to lose again!
Hey, Reagan . . .

Hey, Ronnie! We know it's come to that do-or-die time, baby!
And we know — the Eight Shoes know — that you're gonna do it and die it, baby! And we love ya! And we wish ya good luck!

> Hey, Ronnie! Ronnie!
> Ro-on-neee-eeeee!!

AFTER THEIR BIG OPENING, THE SHOES RELAX, UNDO THEIR BOW TIES AND AD LIB:

SHOES: "Reagan, Reagan, Reagan — now you're the man!" We're going to his inauguration. Leaving now! And you're going to drive, Pete!

PETE TAKES TO THE WHEEL. ON EITHER SIDE COME THE VOICES OF SIGNS ALONG THE FREEWAY AS HE DRIVES RELENTLESSLY ALONG AND ONTO THE MOEBIUS EXIT.

THE SIGNS: Freeway. Entrance Only.
Merging busses ahead.
Antelope Freeway — I in a shield — US 10 Alt — Right lanes only.
Computer Village — Time-share your life-style with three other affordable families!
Tudor Nightmare Village — 2-door, 4-door and Mordor living!
Hungry Turtle — Food served with genuine false modesty!
Antelope Freeway — This Lane — Exit Only.
Easy Street Overpass.
American Optimists say "Welcome Home Hostages!"
Lucky Cloverleaf, Arizona — Diesel Gas Food — Next Exit.
Antelope Freeway — one-half mile . . .
Welcome to New Mexico, Home of the Glowing Indian Dumpsite!
Antelope Freeway — one-quarter mile . . .
Gov. J. P. Sartre Lone Star Highway — No Exit next 1000 miles.
Antelope Freeway — one-eighth mile . . .

PETE READS A COUPLE OF BUMPER-STICKERS ALONG THE WAY:

PETE: Bumperstickers, wow! "I sat on Truman's couch." "I wore Truman's clothes." "I slept with Truman's Wife." "Warm Hole Springs, Mo." "NARI KCUF?" Oh, "Fuck Iran!"

SIGNS: Antelope Freeway — one-sixteenth mile . . .

Stinky River, Indiana. Home of the White Pulp Paper People.
Antelope Freeway — one-32nd mile . . .
Black Lung Drive In — Closed for the Winter.
Antelope Freeway — one-64th mile . . .
Lame Duck Parkway Next Right
Maryland Next Left
Virginia Beltway Southbound
Antelope Freeway one-128th mile . . .
Tomb of the Unknown President Visitor Center
Antelope Freeway — one-256th mile . . .

PETE FINALLY PULLS OFF THE ROAD

PETE: Finally! Motel 6 White Flags Over Washington! Say, isn't that H.K. in those Foster Grants?

SIGNS: Motel Motel Motel . . .
Eat Eat Eat Eat . . .
Queen TV Queen TV Queen TV . . .
Color Bed Color Bed Color Bed . . .
Free Sticky Free Sticky . . .
No Vacancy . . .
Vacancy . . .
Appearing Tonite! The 8 Shoes in the Doo-Dah Room!

PETE: I'll go sign us in.

DAVE: Evening sir. Welcome to the only Nice Motel in town. How long will you be with us?

PETE: Just for tonight. We're playing at the Inauguration.

DAVE: OK. Well, you'll find it's very Clean here. Just fill out the card. Cash or charge?

PETE: Could I get you to believe that the four of us could just register as Mr. and Mrs. John Q. for Quincy Smith?

DAVE: Easiest thing in the world, buddy. Nice to have you with us, Mr. and Mrs. Schmidt.

PHIL A:	Hey! Aren't you Mr. and Mrs. Jan Quisling Schmidt from Anytown USA?
PHIL P:	I'm Joe, boy, and this here's Ed.
PHIL A:	Hi, fella!
PETE:	Well, I'm not really Mr. and Mrs. Quisling . . .
PHIL P:	That's OK. I'm not Joe . . .
PHIL A:	And he's not Ed! How about bending a couple in the Doo-Dah Room? If you catch my meaning?
PHIL P:	If you get my drift!
PETE:	Well, thanks, fellas, but I just drove all the way from California . . .
DAVE:	And boy are my jokes tired!
PETE:	Bellboy, can I have my key?
RICH PARKER:	How about "C"?

HE ROLLS INTO "ALPHIE" AND ACCOMPANIES THE PAGEANT. THE TRIO CONFRONTS PETE:

TRIO:	I can tell by the pie on your tie You're an American — well, so am I! Hi, bub! Howdy! How do ya do? And while we're on the subject, And while we're on the subject, And while we're on the subject, How's yer old Wazoo?
PETE:	What's that all about?
DAVE:	What's it all about, Mr. and Mrs. Jin Quong Smong of Anytown USA?

TRIO SINGS (TO "ALPHIE"): What's it all about, Buddy?

DAVE:	Well, it's about this long . . .
PETE:	And it's about that wide . . .
PHIL A:	And it's about This Country about which we're singing about!
PHIL P SINGS:	I was born an Arabian! I was raised by a Mexican! And I'll die an Iranian, in Cubania, with Comedians!
DAVE:	Yes, we've got a lot of everyone in this land of R's.
PHIL P:	And I wish we had some places to put 'em in!
DAVE:	And that's the problem!
Phil P:	So how are you going to fit in, Sr. y Sra. Juan Quexicoatl Esmeeth?
DAVE:	Dontcha know what to do, big fella? Listen to the radio! Those're the songs you're gonna have to memorize to become a citizen . . .
PHILS (SINGING):	This land is made of mountains, This land is made of mud! This land is made of everything For us and Elmer Fudd — hehehehehe!! This land has lots of trousers . . . Zzipp! This land has lots of bowsers . . . Yip yip yip! This land has lots of mowsers . . . Yip yap zap! And Pussy Cats to eat us when The Sun goes down . . . !
DAVE:	Click! There wasn't always a radio to listen to!
PETE:	No. First they had to bring them from Japan!
PHIL P:	And other places like . . .
TRIO:	Smegma Sirhan Spasmodic Occupied Korea Frog Off Broadway Ho Chi Minh City Exporto Platformo . . .

PHIL A:	And the far-flung Isles of Langerhans!
PETE:	But who were they? What did they look like?
TRIO:	They was small, angry men with hairy faces and burning feces — feet! We was running away from poverty, intolerance, the Army and the Law . . . and the Army . . .
PETE:	And we took them in.
PHIL A:	And they took to us!
PHIL P:	And what do you think they took?
ALL (CHANTING):	Gold from Canada! Oil from Mexico! Geese from their neighbors' backyard! Boom Boom! Mazola from the Indians! Cleveland from the Indians! New England from the Indians! New Delhi from the Indians!
PETE:	Indiana for the Indonesians!
DAVE:	No!
PHIL P:	And that means Veteran's Day!
PHIL A:	But that wasn't enough. We couldn't do it alone! We needed the Hope, the Faith, the Prayers, the Fears . . .
DAVE:	The Sweat, the Pain, the Votes, the Beers!
PHIL P:	The broken bones . . .
DAVE:	The broken phones . . .
PHIL P:	The total integration of . . .
PETE:	Who?
PHIL A:	You! El Little Guy!
DAVE:	And across you, "El," we flung one shining steel rail!

PHIL P: All aboard!

THE QUARTET PERFORM "THE PRESIDENTIAL CHOO-CHOO," BEGINNING WITH THE TRAIN STARTING AND CONTINUING TO A HOOTING STEAMWHISTLE...

ALL: Rock-a-feller... Rock-a-feller... Franklyn Delano, Franklyn Delano, Harry Truman, Harry Truman, Ike & Nixon Ike & Nixon Ike & Nixon, Kennedy/Johnson Kennedy Johnson, Nixon/Kissinger, Nixon/Kissinger... Ford! Ford!

NOW THE TRAIN RUNS SMOOTHLY UNTIL IT HITS A HIGH POINT AND THEN BRAKES WITH A HUSH OF STEAM...

ALL: Reagan! Bushhhhhhh...

DAVE: So how about that, Mr. Bleeding Heart Baby Killer?

PHIL P: Mr. Libertarian?

DAVE: Mr. Devo?

PHIL P: What have you done for any of US lately?

PETE: Well, I...

PHIL A: Mr. and Mrs. Jamal Quafir Smyth! Go to the People! Ask the hands that serve the machines of America! Ask all those thousands of folks who wouldn't say No! to yesterday and Yes! instead of knowing it all!

PHIL P (SINGS): Ask the Postman! Ask the Mailman! Ask the Milkman, white with foam!

PETE: Mr. Authority Figure, what makes America great?

QUARTET: It's candied apples and ponies with dapples
You can ride all day! Hey hey!
It's girls with pimples and cripples with dimples
That just won't go away! Go away!
It's spicks and wops and n-words and kikes
With noses as long as your arm!
It's micks and chinks and gooks and geeks

And honkies — Honk honk!
Who never left the farm . . .
(CHANTING AND FADING OUT)
Farm farm farm farm . . .
Never gonna leave . . . never gonna leave . . .

DAVE: That's America, buddy! Just you remember, Abe Lincoln never did die in vain — he died in Washington DC,

PETE: I see.

DAVE: No, DC! Right here, you dumb Bozo!

PETE: Well, who are all of us Bozos, anyway?

PHIL P: We're one of you, and you're one of us . . . I think.

DAVE: Possibly. Maybe . . . Could be . . .

PETE: I think I know! I know my family! (HE SINGS:)

My sister Polly Esther lives on Three Mile Street.
Looked up in the want ads,
But there was nothing left to eat.
She couldn't pick no cotton
'Cause she didn't know what it was.
She couldn't be a Mammy
'Cause she wouldn't take the bus!
She had to Jump Down, Spin Around,
Pick a bale o' Dacron!
She gotta Jump Down, Spin Around,
Pick some Nylons too!
She gotta get down to Computer College
'Cause there's nothin' else to do!

My brother Otto Matic owns a pickup truck.
He smuggles filter cigarettes
To make a buck.
Couldn't join the Army
'Cause he didn't have the brains.
Couldn't get on TV
'Cause he wouldn't hijack planes!
He had to Jump Down, Spin Around

>Pick a bale o' Dacron.
>He had to Jump Down, Spin Around
>Get some Nylons too!
>He gotta get down to Computer College
>'Cause there's nothin' left to do!
>
>My name is Mr. Occupant. I've seen it on my mail.
>I'm waiting for my whiplash check
>'Cause there's some toot for sale.
>I'd like to be a waiter,
>But just how long can I wait?
>If they paid a man to party
>I'd retire at twenty-eight!
>But hey — I gottta Jump Down, Spin Around . . .

DAVE: They didn't ask questions like that, and they didn't have personality conflicts like that back in 1776! Back in 1776, boy, they were too busy singin' songs like . . .

TRIO: DRUMBEATS UNDER SONG

PHIL P: Yankee Doodle won the war
Using French munitions.
The English marched with German bands,
But zey vere bat musicians!

PETE: That's right! We won in 1776! We won in 1783, and we won in 1794, and we won in 1812, and we won in Mexico . . .

DAVE: But in 1865 we finally found an enemy worthy of us.

PETE: Ourselves!

PHIL P (SINGS): John Brown's body lies a mol'drin' on the ground . . . (HUMS UNDER)

DAVE: Hey, Johnny! I think I found somethin'!

PHIL A: What?

DAVE:	It's a body.
PHIL A:	Is it alive?
DAVE:	No, it's dead!
PHIL A:	And it's a-molderin'!
DAVE:	Phew!
PHIL A:	What's his name?
DAVE:	John Brown.
PHIL A:	That's my name!
DAVE:	Mine too!

MUSIC COMES MARCHING IN

PA:	(LISTENING) Oh, oh! Union musicians!
PHIL (SINGS):	No one came marching home again, no way, no way . . .
PHIL A:	That's right! Nobody came home except President Rutherford B. Hives, who climbed to the top of the Statue of Liberty and said, "Give me your tired, your poor, your huddled masses yearning to make cars — and we'll all make bucks together!"
PHIL P:	Moola, moola! Boola, boola!
DAVE:	The year was 1918. Another President, President Woodrow Whitehouse, promised the Nation . . .
PETE:	"We will not go to war! We will go to war — Over There!

TRIO (AS A BROKEN RECORD): Pack up your buddy in a body bag and smile smile smile CLIK . . . Over there, over there, and we won't come back CLIK and we won't come back CLIK 'e won't come back CLIK ZZZZITTT!

DAVE: But by 1944, auf Deutschland, we were almost all over, uber dere . . .

PHIL P (SINGS LIKE MARLENA) Dropping those bombs again, couldn't help myself . . . Dropping those Clowns again, winning World War Two. Dropping Clowns on you! I can't take it!

THE PHILS SING "OH, BLINDING LIGHT" SOFTLY BEHIND THE SCENE

PETE: So long, Gramma. I got my orders from the government — collect — and I got only ten minutes to leave town.

DAVE: It's going to be dangerous, sonny.

PETE: Only the food, gramma.

DAVE: What's this badge on yer uniform, sonny?

PETE: That's the 101st Fighting Clowns emblem. See him smile? And it says our motto — "Semper Humorous" — Always a laff!

DAVE: What are they gonna do with ya, Donny?

PETE: Well, they drop us at night without a parachute, holding on to a humugus big watermelon. It confuses the radar into thinking we're 500-pound bombs.

DAVE: Oh, oh. Better leave me a picture, Bucky. You're not gonna be back for a long time.

PHIL A: And he wasn't!

PHIL P: 'Cause after they dropped him on Dunquerque, they dusted him off . . .

DAVE: And dropped him on Dussledorf. And then they dumped him out over Dresden . . .

PHIL A: And doped him up and dove him into the D. M. Z.!

QUARTET: Oh, let's paint a tear
For the brave Fighting Clowns!

	Pushed out of the airplane They fall to the ground! Their arms round their melons They salute us with pride! Their shoes all inflated, They fell down and died!
PETE:	So that's who US am! We're all Bozos on the Bus!
PHIL A:	That's right, kid! There's enough watermelons in this country for everybody!
PETE:	Shoulder to shoulder!
DAVE:	That's right!
PETE:	Heart to heart!
PHIL P:	You said it, kid!
PETE:	Satchel to Page!
PHIL A:	You got it! Sound off!
QUARTET CHANTS:	We're bringing the war back home, Where it ought to have been before! We'll kill all the bees! And spiders and flies! And we won't play in iceboxes Lying on their sides! You ain't got no friends on the Left! You're right! You ain't got no friends on the Right! You've left! Sound off! 4 – 3 – 2 – 1 – Zero! Let's march!
PHIL A:	And then, it was all over for everyone but the poor parents, like me, stuck here with an empty whisky bottle full of memories, waitin' for my boy Ronnie to appear. Oh, God! Will he ever come walkin' down that dusty road again . . . ?

PETE: Dad! Dad! It's me! I'm back from the War Movies!

PHIL A: Ronnie, my brave boy! It is you! You're back, and you're almost in one piece! And is this a medal on your chest, my boy?

PETE: In a way. It's a promotional patch for my newest movie, "Fighting Clowns."

PHIL A: Is that what you were doin' over there? Promotin' our way of life? How did you do it?

PHIL P AND DAVE HUM THE "FIGHTING CLOWNS SONG" UNDER

PETE: Well, they dressed us up in clown clothes, took us up in airplanes late at night and pushed us out without any parachutes, strapped to humungus great watermelons. It confused the enemy radar. They thought we were dropping Care packages to the black troops.

PHIL A: That sounds like something our government would do. And if we was seein' this in one of yur movies, like right now, what kind of scenes would be super-imposed over our faces?

PETE: Well, first they dropped us on Berlin — SPLAT — then they bandaged us up and dropped us on Bataan — SPLAT- then they body-bagged and gagged us and dropped us on Big Bien Phu — SPLAT — and then they bungled my contract and dropped me on the back B-lot at Warner Brothers — SPLAT — and finally they bamboozled everybody and dropped me right into the Big Seat!

PHIL A: You mean — in the Big House?

PETE: Yes. The White House.

PHIL A: And what are you this time, Ronnie? Are you the Good Guy or the Bad Guy?

PETE: I'm both. I'm President.

PHIL A: My boy — President of the Untied Snakes...

PETE: Yes, I'm Mr. P now, Dad — and it's really a big job. It's a bigger job on a bigger show than I've ever done before. It's bigger than fakin' the Sports. Bigger than bein' a mouthpiece for GE — and that was a tough one. I had to learn two letters for that one, and they weren't even the same letters! And acting behind all those mules on "Dead Valium Days" wasn't easy either, but that's nothin' compared to my run as President. Now, I'm gonna be everywhere, all at the same time. I'm one of the Presidential Heads In Butter now. Part of my own history, and I'm gonna make it all mine. Sure — they say I'm only a puppet (HE DEMONSTRATES), but I wanna be more than Ronnie Doodie, your "Howdy" President. I want to represent you all — not just the wealthy, but the privileged — those who can afford to wear LIVE fur coats — those of you who have recently inherited tax-free funds. And I'm gonna need everybody's help! I'm gonna need all the help I can get...

>   Hey, Reagan! Reagan! Reagan!
>   You're not too old — old — old!
>   And it's never too late
>   To lose again!
>   Hey, Reagan! Reagan! Regan!
>   You're not too gray — gray — gray!
>   And it's never too late
>   To fade away!
>   Hey, Reagan! Reagan! Reagan!
>   He-e-ey, Reagan!
>   Wa-hoo! Wa-hoo!

CHAPTER 9
SAUCER!

The New Year began at 2 AM on HBO — "The Madhouse of Dr. Fear" premiered. *I thot I looked good — PA too. I wonder where that program is today?*

Phil Austin and I began work on "Saucer!" on Monday, January 5th. We wanted to watch a bunch of movies — after all, this was a flat-out parody we'd been hired to write. It wasn't easy to watch any given film in 1981, most VHS transfers were from film that had long gone dead in the can. Allen Daviau, our DP on "Everything You Know is Wrong," (soon after, Oscar Nominee for "E.T.") had a TV print of "Invaders From Mars." *Lots of laffs & funny ideas — sat around table in clutter of electronic gear — 1939 World's Fair TV in heavy mahogany in the next room. Drank beer in the late aft heat of H'wood winter & watched 1953 unroll.*

It was a workaday Hollywood life. Phil Proctor put me up at his Beverly Hills pad, Austin and I worked in an office at Crossroads of the World on Sunset. Breakfast at Schwab's Drugstore's counter. The Fun House of Mirrors that Hollywood keeps behind the false-front sets in abandoned warehouses allowed us to enjoy the irony that our office — *room 707, is just down the hall from a FICTITIOUS private eye's office — a remnant of "10-Speed & Brownshoe,"* an unlamented 1980 TV series with Ben Vereen.

By the end of the first week's work we had the "Story Outline." *It's a rip-off of "Invaders From Mars" but that's all right — it's got 2 or 3 potentially new ideas, and who knows what will come out of the writing.* Firesign had a date in Huntington Beach at a club called The Golden Bear on the weekend of January 16-17. The acts coming in around us included Captain Beefheart, Tower of Power and José Feliciano. Although we had a sold-out first show, the second was much quieter. *I had a feeling of blankness from some people at both shows.*

The second night *we had a scare that the club was being held up — it was a couple of people carrying guns who got caught in the liquor search. PA locked us in the dressing room for a while before we actually found out was happening.*

Two weeks later, we were guests at a Sherlockon event — a Music Hall — and performed "The Giant Rat" for the first time in years. *Our little show, put together over a beer beforehand, came off ok & we got a great response — partly, I'm sure on our rep, but also because it was funny stuff, & we were in comp. control of the situation. Much autographing & chatter after — including a wonderful drunk who "just hoped I had a day job."*

Ronnie's Inauguration, Super Bowl XV (Raiders won), the gala return of the hostages from Iran — that was January. The Santa Barbara house was about to be empty again as Tinika was wanted back in No Fuck Virginia as the rep theater's costumer. I was comfortable at Proctor's — indeed, I hardly saw him as he was shooting on a National Lampoon movie — it must have been "Class Reunion."

By February, Phil and I were working hard toward the end of the actual screenplay. I thought, *one hears so many stories of films w/un-finished scripts — films w/no scripts — films w/2 or 3 scripts — I won't feel too confident abt this one until we have some feedback — it seems disjointed & disconnected to me now — "fresh ripped" — but I think I know it's funny.*

At the same time, *the tour seems to be shaping up — we have a New Hamp U date on 3/20 — but must get at least a couple more to confirm — then fill in. Could be east mid-May to mid-April.*

We had a meeting with Kim Jorgensen, who liked the script, *looking out over the Strip — Chateau — old Garden of Allah, Pandora's Box — talked — Kim had meeting with Joe Dante, who also liked it — wanted larger frame of ref for threat, more scares, more monsters. Kim was most doubtful abt the "physical characterizations" — and we'll have to work on that to get just what we want.*

We had another meeting, this time with ICM agent Jim Wyatt (who went on to head the William Morris Agency until "deposed"). *Very icy at the top — but he gave FT advice — complete re-write — or even another script — even a script for someone else — in other words he wants a new script — at least a full rewrite of Odyssey in some other form.* PA and PP have been discussing a "parody of muscle-man movies" as an option.

Then we went downstairs to another set of agents and an *extraordinarily affable mtg abt the tour.* The agents were hot for us to go on the road, Proctor had been holding out, *but he was really overwhelmed by the turn of events.* Enthusiasm was once more in the air. Our second draft of "Saucer" was on, the check was in the mail, we were going on the road. *I felt bad as we parted ways at the front door of ICM — not as bad as last Sept — but kinda sad — here were the 2 halves of TFT going their separate ways — & yet, for the first time, the group had not broken up.*

My next life was hinted at, maybe in fact begun, at a "Star Wars" party for NPR's radio version, done using all the movie sound and music and much of the cast. *Socializing for biz w/Frank Mank, Sam Holt, John Bos — finally a useful contact.* Yes, yes . . . they were the trio that hired me and fired me and left me without credit for the Peabody Award my creation "The Sunday Show" won in 1982.

Hollywood writing sessions have to be interrupted at the wrong moment by lonely associate producers, it's the rule. As we were in the last days of our all-important re-write, a guy named Doug and some other guy named Auromy interrupted us — *Doug was clearly in a power-play w/Auromy — representing the 1st draft as an "outline" & vigorously & vulgarly giving us his notes — which we'd really heard already. It was another bizarre movie mtg — I'm sure he thot he was H Cohn to our Pat Hobby. But — even so — was very positive — they* DO *intend to make the picture — or some picture, because Joe Dante is on a pay-or-play deal for his next flic. Also (said Doug) because AVCO wants to get out of a B-horror run and (here's the ringer) because his and Auromy's jobs depend on it. (I doubt that — I'm glad my future doesn't entirely rest on this, or on any one thing. It was all quite a play, & isn't it anyway?)*

Meetings are the stuff of Hollywood. It's where all the games are re-played and all the scenes acted out again. We had one at Disney with Tom Wilhite, who was VP in charge of production then and President of Hyperion Pictures since. It was to pitch *"The Odyssey" & a NDanger idea — it went well — he was a nice fellow in a non-cokey environment — the lot was preserved from 1940 — a lot of old-timers about. Phil and I sold the ideas well & the 4 of us were smooth together. Who knows?*

The Ides of March rolled in again as Austin and I finished the rewrite of the First Draft Screenplay and the four of us puzzled out the touring show and its considerably altered content. We were about to experience the first Full Moon on the Spring Equinox in a hundred years. Perhaps it would be a Fool's Moon too, and bring us the light and laffs we needed.

FADE IN:

EXT. THE UNIVERSE

A dazzling star-field.

Dramatic, ominous MUSIC.

      NARRATOR
     (like Carl Sagan)
  Space. Endlessly threatening.
  Blank. Empty. No light. No
  air. No gravity. Nothing.

We MOVE through the star-field, passing great fireballs.

> NARRATOR
> (continuing)
> Billions and billions of distant suns, infinitely burning. Their planets, bleak, cold, inhospitable. Billions and trillions of miles of nothing at all.

We MOVE past a solar system.

> NARRATOR
> (continuing)
> Let's just look at the facts. Life? Out here? Don't get your hopes up. Think about it — what would it look like? Like this?

CUT TO:

EXT. THE PLANET MONGO

The MUSIC suddenly is heroic, Wagnerian.

Against an exotic extraterrestrial fantasy landscape, with two suns in a lavender sky, a battle is taking place. PRINCE FRAZETTA, a muscular boy in loincloth and arm-bands, biceps bulging, is holding off an elephant-sized dragon — THE GROK — which is threatening the PRINCESS LUR-LINE. The Prince's light sword is making the dragon HOWL. The Princess lies in a faint, bulging out of her scanty golden costume. Her long, golden knife, studded with gems, lies beside her outstretched arm. An EXPLOSION nearby.

> PRINCE FRAZETTA
> Back to the cold fires of Grok-El, from which you sprang, oh Hideous One!

Another EXPLOSION, next to the Princess. Coming to, she sees an approaching menace. Gripping her knife, she runs to the Prince.

> PRINCESS
> (terrified)
> The "Force" is coming!

> PRINCE FRAZETTA
> All is not lost! We can still die together!

The Princess picturesquely drapes herself around the Prince. The dragon ROARS hideously and spits fire. The random EXPLOSIONS increase. The wind rises, plastering the Princess' costume to her beautiful body.

> PRINCESS
> Most noble Prince! I will love you
> beyond death itself!

All seems lost as:

A DREAMY, SMOKEY DISSOLVE TO:

EXT. THE UNIVERSE

We MOVE PAST the solar system and into space.

> NARRATOR
> Not very likely. Wishful thinking.
> The facts are nowhere near so attractive.

With a BURST of menacing electronic MUSIC, a shape looms darkly overhead. It is a huge flying saucer, black and evil. It moves overheard, vibrating and HUMMING.

The MAIN TITLE — a single word — SAUCER! is spelled out right to left in computer print, LED lettering, exclamation point first.

The fact is, Phil and I really wanted to cast Carl Sagan, astronomer, cosmologist and all-around Smart Guy to be in "Saucer!" He would play Cosmo, owner of "The Observatory" — a burger pit with "Out of this World Eating." Sagan's PBS series, "Cosmos," had run in 1980 and was wildly popular. He was just the Name we needed.

We'd also added a few more monsters, including a giant man-eating taco, for Joe Dante, lots more explosions and a part for Jerry Lee Lewis, singing his new hit, "Boppin', Bangin', Blastin' to the Moon!" The screenplay was off, saucering into the Jaws of Hollywood. Swallowed or spit out, how could we know?

CHAPTER 10
THE HORRIBLE TOUR

Nothing about the Tour was clear. We gathered pieces from our recent repertoire and tried them out in rehearsal. We were doing the 8 Shoes with a pre-recorded track because, of course, we couldn't afford even our piano player. "The Giant Rat" was in and out. We were scheduled to open March 26 at Nassau Community College, Garden City, Long Island. Not promising!

The Austins were driving from LA with their dogs. I was also going to drive. See the USA . . . these were the days of giant not-so-EZ-Fold highway maps and no GPS. *Drove out of LA north, made some kind of mistake & ended up a bit out of the way in Mojave.* Pushed my way across country, with a stop with friends in Santa Fe, another in Oklahoma City and on as far as I could into Virginia, where I was stopped icy cold by a snowstorm. *Pulled off to the only motel in town — a little place, but ok, & cheap. Choice of "Patton" & "GWTW" on b&w TV. Steamheat groaning. Another 400 miles to go tomorrow.*

They were very snowy miles until it turned to rain near the coast. Tinika and I had our reunion, right in the midst of her busiest time at the theatre, and left a couple of days later for Long Island — *Hol Inn in Hempstead — the pits!* The good news after days on the highway, Joe Dante had said *"any studio in town wld finance this package."* God, I hope we're in.

ICM's cheerful agents had booked a series of what seemed to me to be totally second-rate venues and worse. Travel on the Eastern corridor was difficult, things were hard to find and discouragement set in pretty early.

Our first date, a Thursday, *turned out to be on a campus on the old Billy Mitchell Field — complete w/hangars & parking on the tarmac. Hofstra next door w/new buildings — but our school a 2-yr community college. Kids did OK tho & it was by & large professionally handled, if way below my personal criteria for "theatrical performance."* Have to give that up tho — trade for the opp to reach a fundamentally new audience.

The next night we were booked in New Haven — not at Yale, but the University of New Haven. *It was a total disaster — the poster advertised a movie — Wizards*

— another comic — a very funny guy in a black karate suit who looked like Brando in Apoc. Now — and us. Well, not us exactly — "Firesign Theatre by Proctor-Bergman." PA saw that and hit the roof. Oona furious with the insult (which was very real, but which I'd determined to swallow in the spirit of not being the asshole). PP his usual philosophical self — the pro, regardless. They did supply two bottles of Irish & we cut the show back & then cut it back again. Got a bit drunk — surely not as far gone as the audience, who'd been boozing all thru the movie — did a quick, bright runthru of the Shoes, against a never-ending roar of conversation & disinterest from the 100 or so people in the house — the cafeteria, of course. Did Nick over an even rowdier response & got out fast, check in hand.

Saturday we were back on Long Island, booked into My Father's Place in Roslyn. It was a famous club in the rock world, hosting top names from 1971 to 1987. However famous, *My Father's Place pretty much a dump — P&B felt it had greatly improved since they put a rug on the floor of the damp, dark basement that served as dressing room. Stage barely adequate. Neither show went well. We were forgetful and, frankly, I just wasn't enjoying the dank, messy joint.*

We were booked back to back on Monday (U. of Maryland) and Tuesday (Virginia Commonwealth University). The rain was pelting down in College Park and the performance was in the Student Union, which was *over-heated to the point of collapse. Then — most devastating of all — the monitors in the bldg. began to be full of screams & drama — what happened? I asked. Reagan was shot came the answer. I couldn't believe it — again! What a country! So that brought the mood generally to zero. While the rain fell violently outside, the screens showed the shooting over & over & the reports from the hospital — just a few miles away — the same rain falling there as here — the heat in the bldg. incredible — the sultry temp outside — the spray-painted "a woman was raped here" outside the doors and on a nearby wall.*

I put in a call to John Hartmann, pleading with him to upgrade the dates and make sure our billing was what we'd agreed on. *PB attacked me for being angry all the time & spoiling his desire to just have a good time. It was all very depressing. Lights were 2 follow-spots so that not much COULD be done. It wasn't very good. ND a real problem. The audience gave us more applause as we came in than after we had performed. They were right.*

We got a sweet interview in The Washington Post, sitting at the Psyche Deli in Bethesda. We were promoting all our current projects — album, NPR shows, movies. — and writer Richard Harrington caught a nice bit of Firesign-on-the-road philosophizing:

"In the late '50s and early '60s all the options of the past were still open," says Bergman seriously. "In the '60s, the options of the future opened, and in the '70s both *the future and the past closed. They just stopped, so all you had was the present to deal with."*

"Futureland — closed for repairs," intones Proctor.

"Past rides — closed for lack of interest," Ossman adds.

"Potholes on the freeway of the present," Bergman mumbles.

"Murder in tomorrowland." Like jazz musicians, the Firesign crew — all in their early 40s now — complete or compliment each other's phrases.

"We've been wearing each other's genes for so long," Ossman says.

We had one more show in Richmond, Virginia before opening in New York at Town Hall. Once again the material was re-arranged. *We did Towel Play & Joey, then Shoes & Nick at Midnight. Audiences were super enthusiastic & seemed to enjoy the show.* That was encouraging.

The old Town Hall was beautiful really — *1500 seats in a real B'way style house — good acoustics, crystal chandeliers* — a bit un-repaired, but a landmark now. *The show — pretty smooth — some confusion over the mikes in Towel Play — new order played well. The audience was lovely — a bunch of signs w/our lines appeared at one point. It has become increasingly obvious the importance of doing the old material.*

In Philly the club was called the Bijou Café, *a weird cock-pit of a place.* Oona Austin had been running or calling the sound cues throughout the tour, usually under terrible conditions. Once again we changed the order of the show — *we dropped Towel and opened with Shoes. Her mood was fierce.* Tinika also joined the show for a while, calling the light cues, as she had done back in the Sixties.

Two shows — first went very well — Danger made sense & the audience was friendly. The second show was not helped by a couple of rowdies. The lateness of the hour and the smoke and drink. Smoke esp made my throat raw.

From Philly we headed south in the rain. Went into VA Beach — lots of young folk & hot cars. Numerous clubs open on the main drag. Rouge's a big one — waitresses in slit harem pants — huge sound eqp — a noisy audience of sailors & fans & actors from VSC, (the Virginia Stage Company, where Tinika was working). *We did the cut-down show — only had to do it once — comedians "opened" for us. Adequately treated. Poured rain outside, & some inside too.*

We were booked two nights at The Cellar Door in D. C., a celebrated venue that hosted artists in a *terribly small 163-seat club in Georgetown. Nice people & pretty good audiences — lots of fans & easy access — we were never alone for a minute.* By this time most of us had colds and *smoke in the club awful. Got them to ask for no smoking on Wed.* On our second night I went *down to the club feeling really poorly. Did a TV tape, then lay on the floor while fans, cameras, interviewers & autograph seekers came & went. Then two shows — the 1st was fun — esp Ben — the second a bear.*

I was still knocking on NPR's door on behalf of Firesign — *all those NPR people are so friendly — but pretty much powerless I think.*

Two days after The Cellar Door we were due in Chicago, by way of Columbus. *Got off way South & had to zigzag up through the burned-out, blasted city to the Lakeshore — it's all front, Chicago is. Miles of industry surround all the refuse and collapse — not very attractive. My room looked out on the lake from the 23rd floor — fog on the water & pretty cold. I avoided P&B — saw them come in — loud and bickering — drive me nuts.*

The Park West, still in business after all these years, was a 1920s vaudeville house turned movie theater turned rock and comedy venue in 1977. *A huge place — 750 seats or so — an old theater with a dome, refinished w/lots of gloss & big b&w photos of scantily dressed people. A big & comfortable dressing room. Lots of lights.* It reminded me of the old Kaleidoscope in Hollywood that had once been Earl Carroll's — a famous and glamorous nightclub. We performed there in 1968, revolving on the creaky stage turntable introducing bands no one would ever hear again (Fever Tree?).

The first show was the best of the trip — an excellent audience & a very theatrical show — one that really caused me to wonder abt what I am doing — have decided it's not art, this performing — but work & not to let it bother me that I think its so many cheap laffs and poor (or no) writing. It is so entertaining to the crowds — they go for it so and are so eager — but there's nothing permanent about it — it's so transitory — anyhow, I felt those laffs & that enthusiasm — & played them & enjoyed myself to a point — but never to a peak.

After another show, which suffered from us all suffering our endless colds, I headed West — *got into Council Bluffs after dark — hunted for a motel, had a lousy dinner — off to Nebraska tomorrow.*

We were at Denver's Rainbow Theater — *out in the new suburbs — not a club at all, but a kind of rock theatre w/a good sized thrust stage & some 1400 seats on three sides. It was another sell-out & a very good show — the first complete show since NYC. We ran the Towel Play lines before & it was really excellent. Knew it was the last shot, so had some fun w/Ben Bland — Joey was good — 8 Shoes have hit their stride & ND was as good as it can be, given the writing problems. The audience was excellent — young & old — enjoyed the show greatly.*

It had been three weeks on the road. We expected to climax the tour at UCLA's Royce Hall a few days later, but the show had been cancelled for lack of sales. *That puts a dent in the economics of this trip, for sure.* Somehow the performance was on again by the time I got home to Santa Barbara. It may have been on, but we were off. The Tour was over. What's next?

Firesign in Blackface. Yikes!

THANK YOU, MR. PRESIDENT!

When we played our last dates — "The 15th Anniversary Tour" — we brought back "High School Madness" and continued performing "Frame Me, Pretty," "In The Hot Tub" and "Thank You, Mr. President." The latter script had undergone post-election changes and was regularly improvised on. I played FDR in a wheelchair, Proctor was an acid Truman, Austin the ultimate Nix, and Peter, uncomfortable as Ike, had morphed into a randy LBJ.

The lights come up on FDR snoozing in his wheelchair. The Nix slouches in and sits, as if on a toilet. Truman follows.

NIX: What a wonderful supper! Cold baked beans, catsup, cottage cheese, meatloaf and jelly-babies. I gotta take a wicked shit!

HST: Sonofabitch! which one of you crazy bastards made the dessert? That baked Hiroshima was a blast!

NIX: Don't thank me, Mr. President. I didn't have a fuckin' thing to do with it. Lyndon does the desserts.

HST: (MIXING DRINKS) Well, Hell's bells! It was goddam wonderful! I'm gonna fix us some after-dinner drinks. Franklyn! Wake up, Franklyn, for chrissake! Are we gonna have to wait till he finishes his fourth term before we have cocktails? Franklyn!

FDR: (WAKING) Good evening, gentlemen. Are we going to watch television?

HST: No, Mr. President. We're not going to watch TV, for chrissake! We're going to have a few highballs first, and enjoy this goddamn steambath!

FDR: Oh, darn I thought we WERE going to watch television.

NIX: Shit. There's nothing on. They cancelled the fuckin' football game. Shit!

Harry and FDR are a bit stunned by this, then Harry serves the cocktails. LBJ enters as they drink.

Chapter 10: The Horrible Tour

HST: Bottoms up!

LBJ: At ease, shitheels! [Insert topical joke here.] It's sure been a lot more peaceful around here since Reagan organized those press conferences.

HST: I'll drink to that!

LBJ: I'll drink to anything.

They all drink and Harry gets up to mix another shaker. All four muse (or brood) for a beat, then:

FDR: I like this steambath his wife put in. (TO LBJ) And you, Mr. President. I especially like you. You tried to win the war.

LBJ: Yes. But you started it.

They toast and refill their glasses. Harry is pissed:

HST: But, Mr. Presidents! I dropped the goddam bomb!

IKE: You really gave 'em hell, Harry!

HST: If you can't stand the heat, get out of the steambath!

NIX: Say, Mr. President. Have you got the fuckin' TV Guide?

Another stunned moment. They brood for a beat, then:

HST: We're not going to watch television, Mr. President. We're going to have another goddam highball and I'll play the piano. Do you know "Chopsticks?"

NIX: I never learned to use them.

HST: It's easy. Just jam 'em under your goddam fingernails and play! (HE DOES) See? All these Chinese tunes sound the same.

FDR: (TO LBJ) I never did like him.

LBJ:	Which one?
FDR:	The little one — in the hat. Mean. He never would have been President if it hadn't been for my heart.
LBJ:	And that little honey in the Hot Springs . . .
NIX:	Say, Mr. Presidents — have we eaten dinner yet?
HST:	Well, I sure as hell have. (HE CUTS ONE) I gotta go to the crapper. (GETS UP AND CUTS ANOTHER) So long, Mr. Presidents . . . (LEAVES, CUTTING)
LBJ:	God, I love the smell of napalm in the morning!
FDR:	Ah, yes. Like mustard gas and dead horses. Makes me hungry just to think about it.
LBJ:	Well, I gotta go pour some bar-be-que sauce on my pecker and heat up ol' Lady Bird. Don't start any secret wars without me, pardners!

LBJ leaves and FDR watches the brooding Nix for a beat, then:

NIX:	Do you know what I like? Ask me.
FDR:	What do you like?
NIX:	Big legs.
FDR:	I had big legs once . . .
NIX:	Big old, thick old, meaty old, great big old, meaty old, big old nylons and big old heels and big old, big old legs! I remember the little things, too. The way there always used to be something to eat late at night. Damn, that Ike could make great pastries. And that lady in Erlichman's office — the one with the flat-top and those tremendous boobs! The rest of it might as well've been a dream, just a dream . . .

Nix drifts off-stage, leaving FDR.

FDR: Ciao, Dick. Go to hell, Harry! All the way, LBJ! Now that we're alone, Barbwa, I'd like to tell you about me and Uncle Joe at Yalta. All he wanted was to talk about the Bomb, and all I wanted was his recipe for borsht. You take a lot of beets from the peasants, throw in a handful of reds, and stir 'em up real slow. Now there's a wonderful supper . . .

FDR closes his eyes and the lights fade to black.

CHAPTER 11
THE PINK HOTEL

We were booked into some publicity event that was supposed to take place at the Balloon Races but got moved to the Wax Museum. *They were afraid it would rain, but of course it was a beautiful afternoon. We did the show with Pat Sajak — pleasant, just as he appears on the news —* Pat had been a weatherman on the local NBC station and we always called him "The Cookie Man" because, somehow, he looked like the storied Gingerbread Man of children's verse. He graduated to Wheel of Fortune and the spinning world of game shows and is one of Hollywood's notorious conservatives.

We did the interview in *a room in the Palace of Living Art — the room with no "nudes" — slick-pussied wax dolls. It was all over by 3 or so — I felt relaxed and comfortable. We got a quick tour thru the Wax Museum — it was truly incredible — 3D kitch.*

Peter and I had another date in Columbia Missouri for the Midwest Radio Theatre Workshop. We taught radio technique and produced a live four-play broadcast that introduced one of my "old radio" pieces, "Maxwell Morgan, Crime Cabby." Many of the participants in MRTW became lifelong friends, including my favorite radio character actor, Richard Fish. The Workshop was a four-day high and very collaborative, which characterizes the "Firesign Technique."

Mid-May. We met with a guy from Warner Bros. Records. *He allowed as how he was pleased we were all healthy — god knows what he expected — Quaalude dropouts? And also that we really WANTED to do an album impressed him.* He'd get back to us in a couple of weeks. Nothing to do but wait it out.

In Isla Vista, home to UCSB, artists Harry and Sandra Reese had a very small hand-set-type press — Turkey Press. Harry, smitten by my thick scrapbook of notes, drawings, funny names and weird dialogue, pulled a selection out and made the "Bozo Book," each a one-of-a-kind original and the rarest of Firesign "collectables." At the same time, Sandra designed three beautiful small books and a poem on cards called "Hopi Set." Treasures, elegantly capturing many of the works I'd read live on early Firesign radio shows.

By mid-August I was back in hot, smoggy LA, working on a script for the new album — at least on a short piece of in-studio production we could use as a demo for the real 40–minute thing. We had two studio days. *I never left the building from the time I got in — 10:15 until the end of the session 10 hrs later. It went very slowly, w/much rewriting & searching for characters — PB was last aboard & in fact was in an "I don't understand this" mood that is always a drag — meaning "I haven't done my homework, so now we all have to do it." PP & PA in one snit — PP giving an insecure PA line readings — some jealousy on P&B's part to me and PA for starting the piece, perhaps.*

We recorded and re-recorded the 1st scene — finally getting it in two parts — the action flowing well & the voices coming. Had barely time to talk thru the 2nd scene when studio time was over. So we got just over 3 mins, unsweetened, in 10 hrs. I don't know how much we'll be able to get done in the time available — probably not the three written scenes.

Our next session was at night — *we only worked until midnight* — did the 2nd scene rather faster than the 1st. Enjoyed it very much on the listen-back. Did a few effects & called it a night. It began to sound like "Raiders" & even PB got into it more.

The script that follows is a transcript of the recorded demo for the first two scenes, with the script we didn't record for the third. It was definitely going to be a "Raiders of the Lost Ark" movie embedded in a new computer game. A very solid Firesign Theatre concept.

THE PINK HOTEL BURNS DOWN or, What Good Is A Halfling in a Holocaust?

An entirely new audio comedy by
THE FIRESIGN THEATRE

Summer 1981

Produced by Phil Austin & Fred Jones
Special Audio Effects by Fred Jones

*

"The war was an acceptable delusion."
July 14

"What's that smell?"
"I don't know — dragon's breath?"
"Always give the monster an even break."
July 15

43 BREAKTHRU
One must resolutely make the matter known at the court of the King. It must be announced truthfully. Danger.
July 27

"The Sonofabitch, The Dr. & The End of the World"
Script title, July 28, 1981

PLAYERS OF THE LOST ART

Armistice "Army" Brooks is one player in the game. So are Old Grizz the Leatherback, Earl The Halfling and the awesome Dustmaster.

In the spirit of the latest in legendary heroes and high adventure — inspired by the challenging new video and computer games of mystery and fantasy — The Firesign Theatre invites you to be a Player too, but look out! Once you're in the game, there's no telling where the next Danger will come from.

*

SIDE ONE — "THE ROAD TO BONUS CITY"

First Move — "You Wake Up In The Pink Hotel"

SOUND:	HEARTBEATS
GAME:	Good morning, Player Number One. You wake up in the second best room in the Pink Hotel. You have survived the effects of the banquet, but you cannot move your left hand. There is a door on the East wall, opposite your bed. And next to it is a picture of a naked Devil in the mirror.
ARMY:	He looks terrible. Who is that?
GAME:	It's you.
ARMY:	It's me. I look terrible. Where are my jeans?
GAME:	Inside your body.
ARMY:	No, I mean my trousers.
GAME:	Your trousers are on the chair against the South wall.
ARMY:	I get up, I go to the chair. I'll put on my pants and get out of here.
SOUND:	HIS MOVEMENTS. A CRASH.
ARMY:	Ow! Ow! What happened?

GAME:	You knocked over the champagne bottle.
ARMY:	I pick up the bottle. I pick up the . . . Why can't I pick up the bottle?
GAME:	You cannot move your left hand.
ARMY:	I'll use my right hand . . . Is there anything left?
GAME	There is one drink left.
ARMY:	Good. Save it.
GAME:	Saved.
ARMY:	OK. Now — give me my trousers.
SOUND:	SNAKE HISS.
ARMY:	Help! Help!
GAME:	There's a one-eyed snake in your trousers.
ARMY:	I hate snakes. Give him the champagne.
SOUND:	SNAKE DRINKS, HICCUPS AND DROPS BOTTLE.
GAME:	The snake is now drunk.
ARMY:	Ah, good. I'll hold onto it.
GAME:	Saved.
SOUND:	KNOCK ON DOOR.
ARMY:	What's that?
FLIPPER:	(MUFFLED)
GAME:	A muffled voice calling for help.
ARMY:	I'm coming. I put on my pants.
GAME:	Saved.

ARMY: I go to the door.

SOUND: KNOCK KNOCK KNOCK.

ARMY: Open the door — with my right hand — and I step out . . .

SOUND: DOOR OPENS. FIRE EFFECTS IN BACKGROUND.

[BACKGROUND FOR FIRE SEQUENCE:

SOUND: SIRENS, HELICOPTERS, WATER HOSES.

DISTANT VOICES: Jump! Jump!

OTHER VOICE: Do not jump! We will get to you in a few days! There are people ahead of you!

ANOTHER VOICE: Disregard alien orders! Don't listen to those people from the Italian film crew. Do not jump!

ITALIANS: Hey! Americani! This way!

US TV ANN: So that's what's happening here, live. And the sight of all those boats with the black candles at helm and stern is really nothing, compared to . . .

VOICES: The sky Bridge is falling! The Hotel is on fire!]

ARMY: Ooooh! . . .

FLIPPER: Army! Army! Hey, buddy! Don't close the door! Oh, no! We're trapped out here and the hotel's on fire!

ARMY: Where's the Rain Queen?

FLIPPER: I traded her to the Dustmaster.

ARMY: For what, Flipper?

FLIPPER:	For this fine lump on my back. Meet Earl The Halfling.
EARL:	Hiya, bloodbag!
ARMY:	What are we going to do with a Halfling in a holocaust?
EARL:	Watch it! I've got a really low level of predictability!
SOUND:	EARL KICKS ARMY
ARMY:	Ow! Earl! He kicked me! I'll kill him!
FLIPPER:	No, no! He carries a Lunchworm with an important message for ya!
ARMY:	Lunchworm, give message.
EARL:	Oh, no — you have to give me something.
ARMY:	What have I got?
GAME:	Inventory. Player One. Half a map of parade route, ghetto blaster, glass key, checkered trousers, schnockered snake, souvenir snowball with the skyline of Bonus City.
ARMY:	I like that. I like all this stuff.
FLIPPER:	Give him the key!
ARMY:	I want all this stuff!
EARL:	Give me the key!
ARMY:	OK. Lose key.
EARL:	Here, Boss.
FLIPPER:	Thanks, Earl.
ARMY:	Lunchworm, give message.
LUNCHWORM:	You know, we really must have lunch sometime.

ARMY: That's no message!

EARL: How about — the Sky-Bridge is falling?

FLIPPER: Holy hotcakes! Looks like Game Over, Number One!

ARMY: Stand back! Not while I still have a snake in my pants! I'm just gonna whip it out . . .

[BACKGROUND:

ITALIANS: Jump! Jump! I'm rollin'! Jump towards the light!

FIRE CAPTAIN: We know something's happening, but we don't know what it is!

ITALIAN: Our people are seeing their people about the contract right now!

VOICES: CHEERS!]

ARMY: . . . Tie a knot in it, and lasso that flagpole. (HE DOES SO)

FLIPPER: Go for it!

ARMY: Hop on, Number Two.

FLIPPER: Not this one. I've got a key!

EARL: Save me! Save me!

ARMY: Ow! Earl! Get off my back!

GAME: One and a half players. Too heavy. The snake breaks.

SOUND: SNAKE BREAKING

ARMY & FLIPPER: (FALLING) Aaaaaaaaaaaaaaaaa . . .

EARL:	Suck air, white devil! We halflings fly!
SOUND:	FLAPPING WINGS. DISTANT SPLOOT.

Second Move — The Sub-Rosa Bar

GAME:	The Pink Hotel burns down. Game over. You have accumulated 450 points. You are not a top-ten scorer. Your room has been cleared and is now available. Do you wish to register at the Pink Hotel? (MESSAGE REPEATS)
SOUND:	THE BAR INTERIOR. THE TV IS ON.
[TV SOUND:	RODEO CROWD
JIM:	You know, that cowboy up there on that worm — that's Old Spice he's got his hooks into — well, he's a bartender from the Bronx ...
JACK:	No, Jim. He's a burgher from Bremmerhaven ...
BOB B:	Whoa, boy! No, I think that's wrong, Jack — he's a Bleached Collar Berber from Bonus City's mixed Black, Spanish and foreign stock, in an aging, center-city row of unskilled high-rise areas.
JACK:	Well, he can't ride a sandworm for shit! He's down!
WORM CLOWN:	Hola! Hey! Worm! Guiso! Look at me! When they let you out of the bottle? OK, seriously — two big, ugly worms walk into this bar. Can ya hear me?
WORM:	RRRRRRRR
WORM CLOWN:	And the bartender says, We don't serve slugs here!

WORM:	RRRRRRRR
WORM CLOWN:	And the worm says . . .
WORM:	RRRRRRRR
WORM CLOWN:	I don't want slugs, I want the whole bottle!
WORM:	RRRRRRRR
JACK:	Is he laughing or just passing earth?
JIM:	Same thing to a worm, Jack.
BOB:	Ya know, those big worms are the only species that like to laugh at itself. Ya know, ya try and tell a story about a swarm of hornets comin' into a bar — well, everybody leaves!
JIM:	Speaking of bars, how about a beer?
JACK:	We'll be back to the Mudfly Wrestling Contest from Weteye, California . . .
JIM:	Right after this.
TV ANNOUNCER:	You know, the rules of the game have changed. Today, it's Lo-Water Beer — it can't be the water, 'cause there isn't any. You'll say:
VOICE:	Why is my head so heavy?
VOICE 2:	I don't care if it's sludge, so long as it goes down cold.
ANNOUNCER:	That's Lo-Water, the Heavy Head Beer, from the Dust King Brewing Company, Subrosa, California.]
MEANWHILE:	

GRIZZ: Ah! You're a loser, sonny. First rule — never talk to a Lunchworm.

ARMY: Takes me a little time to figure things out.

GRIZZ: I've played this a thousand times. You break the mirror with the champagne bottle, yell "Yahoo!" and you go straight to the Bridal Suite. Simple as that. Boner City!

ARMY: I'm doin' OK. Existence for me is just one controlled fall after another.

GRIZZ: Yeah? For a guy your age, you've got a low life potential. Ya ever think about Death?

ARMY: Look, old timer, back off, OK?

GRIZZ: I can get rid of that Halfling and take ya right to the Rain Queen.

ARMY: I played it my way.

GRIZZ: If I don't drink beer regular, I achieve real high powers of irritability.

ARMY: Alright, alright. Excuse me.

WE LISTEN IN TO "PUNT," WHO IS HAVING A CONVERSATION WITH HIMSELF.

PUNT: This is the kind of thing I'm talking about — the Italian Masonic Conspiracy! The P-2! Doesn't anyone know what I'm talking about? See this picture?
He's got a hood over his head.
Exactly!
Howja like him to be President?
He IS President!
Don't get smart with me! I started as a kid! Been workin' all my life — basically as a graph figure. For a long time I was a half-child model. You know? Those families that have 2-and-a-half kids? That was me!

GRIZZ: What a geek!

ARMY: Who's that guy talking to, anyway?

PUNT: Lemme tell ya a story . . .
Sylvia, punch me up another gin and sand from the well, wouldja?
Didja hear the one about the two legal Mexicans from Bonus City? They come across a bunch of Sunday Slavics, Young Moneys and Patio Poolers standing around watching a couple a dogs making magic on the street. These dogs don't need air-conditioning! You know what I mean?

GRIZZ: Aw, shut up!

PUNT: Hey! I've got Multiple Identity. Lay off. A guy's taking me to dinner tonight. (Me too. Not me.) The Canned Soup Shack, OK?

GRIZZ: Say, fella! Don't drop your money inta that Dustmaster! You don't wanna play alone — bad trip! Get me another beer!

ARMY: I like to play by myself.

SOUND: COIN IN SLOT IN GAME. DOOR OPENS AND DUST STORM BLOWS AS FLIPPER ENTERS.

FLIPPER: Sons of the Wind! Children of the Sand! Old Dustmaster's back and I'm dry as the wormcast on a full sprung Chevy. Lo-Water Beer all around! Drinks on the Caravan! Leaves in a half hour. See me to join up. I've got the wind-maps! Better than Government Goof-Sheets. The rates go down when the wind goes down. How 'bout you, Player? You goin'?

ARMY: Sorry, I'm drivin' alone.

FLIPPER: Alone! You ever see what your average Sister does to a car? Eats it down to the chrome on the tailpipe! You can see through everything but the windshield.

ARMY:	I heard I could get a Troll to guide me.
FLIPPER:	Guide ya to the Chop Shop. Make car suey outa yer Caddy! How about it, 450? Clock's runnin'.
ARMY:	Nope. I'll ride with the risk. Valiant's right out front . . .
FLIPPER:	The one with the California plates say GAME-OVR?
ARMY:	You got it.
FLIPPER:	Not me. They got it.
ARMY:	Who got it?
FLIPPER:	A couple a Trolls from Edible Wrecks Garage.
GRIZZ:	You're doomed, sucker.
PUNT:	(SINGING) Toad away, toad away . . .
GAME:	The Trolls have your car. You have lost 250 points.
ARMY:	Fuck!
GAME:	You are not a top-ten scorer. Do you wish to sign on for the Dustmaster Caravan?
ARMY:	No way!
GAME:	Do you wish to sign on for the Dustmaster Caravan? . . .

Third Move — Edible Wrecks Garage

[BACKGROUND RADIO PLAYS "THE HALL OF THE MOUNTAIN KING." WHEN IT CONCLUDES:

RADIO ANNOUNCER: Well, that was "Hall of the Mountain King," Number One on K-TROL — Troll music for Trolls and people who think like Trolls. Brought to you by Escarfier Car Sauce, now in the easy-to-break bottle. Now, here's Number Two, going out to Ma, Pop and Yo Yo in Troll Country! It's the same as Number One!

THE RADIO CONTINUES TO PLAY UNDER THE SCENE.]

HYDROX: Oh, boy! That's my favorite! Turn it up! Dumdumdumdum . . .

GYGAX: Tear off a piece a that T'bird before it's all gone, Slamdunk.

SLAMDUNK: How about a windwing, Gygax?

GYGAX: Gaaaa! I'm inta innards. Hack off the carburator.

SLAMDUNK: You want the hoses?

GYGAX: Hell, yes. That's the best part.

HYDROX: Gimme that soft, smelly piece.

SLAMDUNK: You mean this here passenger seat, Hydrox?

GYGAX: I donno how you eat that stuff. You don't know who's been sittin' there.

HYDROX: I like the taste of strangers.

SLAMDUNK: What's for desert?

GYGAX: How 'bout the taillights off that '65 Valiant?

SLAMDUNK: Yum! Pour on the 30-weight!

ARMY: (FROM OFF) Hey! Hey, in there? Anybody gonna help me or what?

HYDROX: Can'tcha see we're on a lunch break?

THEY ALL LAUGH.

ARMY: There it is! That's my car! What the hell did I do? The goddam meter was fed. It wasn't 4 o'clock yet.

GYGAX: Take it easy. We didn't bring it in.

ARMY: I suppose it drove down here by itself.

THEY AGREE, LAUGHING.

ARMY: OK, who's got my keys?

HYDROX: Not me.

SOUND: HE GLORPS THE KEYS DOWN, BELCHES AND JINGLES.

GYGAX: Can't release the car without registration.

ARMY: It's in the glove-box, in the car.

SLAMDUNK: That'll be another fifty.

ARMY: On toppa what?

GYGAX: Let's see your license.

ARMY: It's in my wallet, in my coat, in the trunk.

HYDROX: Can't open no trunk without no keys. That'll cost ya.

GYGAX: Unless you're a Wizard. Open it with a spell.

ARMY: Never could spell.

GYGAX: Let's eat it before it spoils.

ARMY: I'll spoil you, you little dwarf! Here, try this headlight for a head-size!

SOUND: HE CRASHES IT DOWN.

HYDROX: He crushed Gygax! Hand me those pliers, Slamdunk!

ARMY: How about the whole friggin' toolbox?

SOUND: A HUGE CRASH AND CLATTER

SLAMDUNK:	This fist am gonna drive you a hundred miles through the floor!
ARMY:	Of course, mileage may vary!
SOUND:	BIG FIGHT. THE VALIANT STARTS UP AND DRIVES AWAY.
ARMY:	Hey! Bring my car back!
SLAMDUNK:	Gaaaaa!
SOUND:	HE CRASHES TO THE FLOOR.
ARMY:	Yahoo!
GAME:	You win the fight. Your car is still missing, again. You are not a top-ten scorer. Do you wish to sign on for the Dustmaster Caravan? Do you wish to sign on for . . . (REPEATS, FADING)

TO BE CONTINUED

CHAPTER 12
WASHINGTON, D.C.

Labor Day came and went. Austin called to say there was a favorable memo at Universal about "Saucer!" and urged we release "Pink Hotel" on Rhino if no one else was interested. I was playing my cards with NPR — there was apparently a job in Washington DC — and got my resume off. Rumors continued about tour dates. I got a script-writing job — a radio version of David Ives' story "Homo Obliteratus" which turned out to be a solo performance piece for me.

Otherwise, I felt a bit obliterated myself. None of Firesign's two years of writing and performance seemed to be what anyone wanted in the Eighties. Peter's interests were always divided and he adored showing up and Wizarding at conferences of medical people or the new technologists. Phil Proctor was moving back into the Hollywood world after years of frustration with the collaboration. Who could blame him?

As Firesign's Anniversary month of October rolled around, I finally got a response to our album demo — *the schmuck from WB called in the eve to confess he'd LOST! the Pink Hotel tape & hadn't found it until this week. I really couldn't believe it! So he called to say he liked it a lot & that it filled the bill & was playing it for people — including a couple of A&R men who didn't "know what it was."*

The "Fall Tour" had manifested, billed as our "15th Anniversary Tour," and comprised of San Diego and San Francisco. The powers-that-be at NPR had "posted the job" — *they will interview & make their selection by the end of 1st week of Nov. I expect I'm still up in the running. I'll have to ask TFT for a leave of absence — nobody quits!*

By mid-month we'd set the show via conference call. *PB was anxious to go, PP matter-of-fact. PA seemed easy.* NPR called back *to say that they wanted me to come there for discussion, & so I'll go in between gigs, which is perfect, if hectic, timing. So that's perking hot now & makes me a bit spacy to think about.*

I drove back and forth from Santa Barbara, meeting with the boys, planning out the run of the show, gathering costumes, working well together. *Everyone in good spirits. PP doing a Taco Bell ad today.*

Our Saturday night show in San Diego was on the UCSD campus and had been arranged by Jerome Rothenberg, an old friend from New York poetry days. We were part of a colloquium on "The Oral Mode in Contemporary Art and Culture" and all went smoothly. *A full and very warm house, to my delight & surprise. Oona congratulated us at the end — an especial compliment from her. A good high after the show. All wished me well on this job hunt — even Oona said to have a good time. PB said that my getting the job might be just what TFT needs. I wonder what* WILL *happen . . .*

We were part of a panel on improvisation on Sunday — *it wasn't much, & things did get tedious after that,* so back home to pack.

I spent four days in Washington. I met with my immediate boss, John Bos and had lunch with Tim Owens, an old friend from SB who was doing an excellent job with NPR's jazz programming. I met three producers already on the line for the unnamed program and the illustrious Jay Kernis, a Peabody Award winner who was senior producer of "Morning Edition." *He bright, passionate about his work. I liked him.*

It was nearly over. Met again with Sam Holt, the programming V.P., had a brief encounter with Frank Mankiewitz, always attired with his PT109 tie clasp, and finally back to Bos to say "yes" to the job. *The job is a major one — everyone in Programming is putting a heavy weight on this show to keep the Dept. going. Morale is low — there is no sense of accomplishment because no one is hitting b'cast deadlines. I come in liked & respected — a celeb.* I was given a choice of positions with the program — Host or Executive Producer. I felt they needed me as producer/creator first and foremost. I could always hire myself as Host when things really developed, or so I thought.

I returned to San Francisco for the last of our performances. We were at the York Theatre, mostly a movie house (we came in between "Nosferatu" and "Endless Love") for three shows, including our 15th Halloween anniversary. A group of comics we knew, The High-Wire Radio Choir, opened for us and we went on with *a sense of this is a "last performance."*

Farewells to TFT. PB promising to get back to NY soon to see me & wanting to do something on the show. PP good-lucking me. PA telling me in confidence it was OK w/P&B that I was going & that he was just going to go on w/TFT ignoring the fact that I'm not in town. I felt good abt all that — it will go on w/out me just fine, as it has done.

Tinika and I took a brief holiday in Mendocino, where Peter had some beautiful property in the woods. We'd spent good times there in the Seventies and friends from the Renaissance Pleasure Faire were in residence.

News from Washington should have given me an insight into the Future: *Sam Holt is not yet giving his approval — has held up the press release — brought me down to earth after the whole bizness seemed to have gone smooth as pork pie. We drove on south to SB where I was on the phone w/Bos a long time, bargaining over how to best get thru to Sam. Told him I wldn't go to Denver to "audition." Just spoke to Ruth Hirschman & she in strong agreement & will go to the mat if my apt. is blocked for political reasons.*

It wasn't. I left for Washington and what was to become "The Sunday Show" on November 10. Hollywood on the Potomac and the snow was soon to fall.

David Ossman is executive producer of THE SUNDAY SHOW from National Public Radio, America's first national radio program dedicated to the arts. THE SUNDAY SHOW premieres on NPR member station on April 4, 1982.

AFTERWORD

It was with great expectations (and real creative relief) that I departed the Firesign for the promise of working again in the audio medium. Back to radio, where I had begun, twenty years before.

The "Boys," as I always thought of them, continued to create work under the Firesign name. With me gone, Austin, the serious surrealist, found himself partnered with P&B, the potent gagsters. To my mind, it never quite worked. It wouldda had some poetry with me in the room. Toward the end of the threesome's collaboration they had access to new, digital technology and created a complex, multi-stacked album cum video game, "Eat Or Be Eaten." It was the right direction and had the depth needed to carry the Firesign name onward.

We four met again, cautiously, a decade after. Everything in my life was different by then. I lived with my wife and partner, Judith Walcutt and our two young boys on Whidbey Island. We were our own production company, producing large audio works for public radio. We were a happy team.

It was Firesign's 25th Anniversary (many rock bands were also celebrating theirs) and we enthusiastically rehearsed fully staged versions of our most popular albums for a show at the Seattle Paramount. It was a sell-out hit. The tour that followed was not. "The Road," always comfortable to P&B, was hardest on Austin, who travelled by van with Oona and their beloved dogs. For me, it was dogged by rewrites and bickering. We returned to radio silence.

As the Nineties were ending Richard Foos and Harold Bronson, the creative and sympathetic founders of Rhino Records came once again to Firesign's rescue. The Millennium was the perfect excuse for a "real" Firesign album — a take on American society and culture as we saw it, plunging fearfully over the Edge of Time. "Give Me Immortality or Give Me Death" and the two following albums were the peers in writing, performance and production of anything we'd done at Columbia in the Sixties and Seventies. The final album, "Bride of Firesign," allowed our most beloved characters — Nick and Rocky, Porgy and Mudhead — to have one last turn together.

Twenty-First Century Firesign also included radio satire for NPR's celebrated "All Things Considered" and twelve two-hour mostly improvised broadcasts for the brand-new XM Satellite Radio. "Fools In Space" was a Gold Medal winner. Our body of work now extended over 35 years.

The financial apocalypse of 2008 (predicted in Firesign's 1999 "Boom Dot Bust" album) brought us back together for a series of modest shows in Washington, Oregon and California, each of which allowed us to dig back into the original quartet of Columbia records and re-present them to an audience of our beloved fans (and their children!). We stood at microphones and held scripts and read aloud. I guess we were saying a long goodbye.

Peter died suddenly, unexpectedly in March 2012. We had spent a year and a half as partners in a new Radio Free Oz blog. That was another return, as so much of later life seems to be, to the roots of the collaboration. Three years later, Phil Austin was suddenly gone. It was over. It was really over then.

But it's never over, my dearly beloveds, and brother Proctor and I will go on being relentlessly silly and repeating our lines until we too have had our day. And we did it all for you, because you needed us to tell you that everything you know is wrong, that we are all waiting for the Electrician, that we are all Bozos on this bus together.

DAVID OSSMAN,
WHIDBEY ISLAND,
OCTOBER 2017

David Ossman (Photo by Jim Carroll.)

We won't judge you
for not having all the
8-tracks.

We don't have them
either.

Get books, CDs, and more
to fill your Firesign
Five-Foot Shelf at
www.FiresignTheatre.com

"Where there's smoke,
there's savings!"

 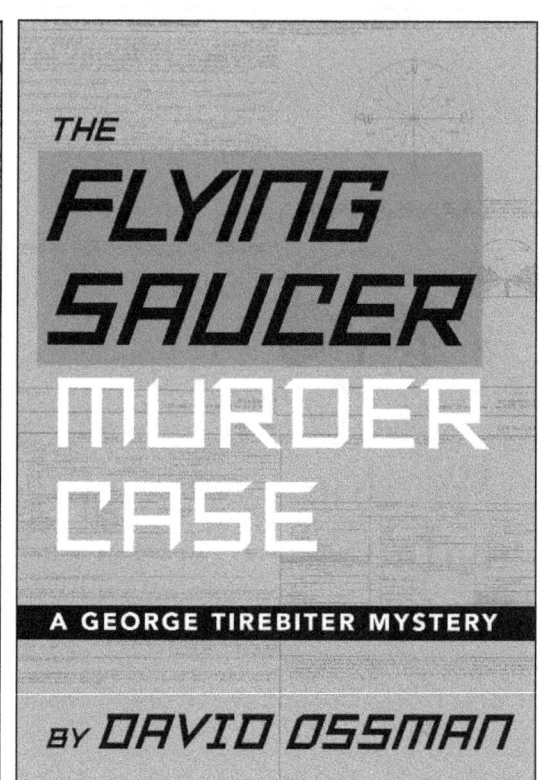

Hollywood, 1945, in the Golden Age of Radio and Movies! George Tirebiter stars in a murder case that can only be solved live On The Air! Silent film glamour, fun with the future president, a secret romance, network radio comedy, all a part of *THE RONALD REAGAN MURDER CASE!*

George Tirebiter, blacklisted, writes sci-fi in 1953 and runs a typical L.A. bungalow court where a saucer-seeker is electrocuted by radio. Burlesque comic Lenny Bruce joins blue Venusians, alien abductors, and the nude model next door, to solve *THE FLYING SAUCER MURDER CASE.*

Ossman's rich period detail is complimented in both volumes by illustrations, notes, an additional short story and features on Tirebiter's career and the long association between author and character. "These are the places I grew up and worked in. They're all gone now. George's adventures let me revisit them and take my readers along with me. It's a top-down ride through the City of the Angels!" Ossman says.

THE TIREBITER MYSTERIES, FROM BEARMANOR BOOKS

www.ingramcontent.com/pod-product-compliance
Lightning Source LLC
Chambersburg PA
CBHW081218170426
43198CB00017B/2652